PENGUIN POPULAR REFERENCE

GERMAN PHRASE BOOK

D0767182

German Phrase Book

SECOND EDITION

Ute Hitchin and
Jill Norman

PENGUIN BOOKS

PENGUIN BOOKS

Published by the Penguin Group
Penguin Books Ltd, 27 Wrights Lane, London W8 5TZ, England
Penguin Putnam Inc., 375 Hudson Street, New York, New York 10014, USA
Penguin Books Australia Ltd, Ringwood, Victoria, Australia
Penguin Books Canada Ltd, 10 Alcorn Avenue, Toronto, Ontario, Canada M4V 3B2
Penguin Books (NZ) Ltd, Private Bag 102902, NSMC, Auckland, New Zealand

Penguin Books Ltd, Registered Offices: Harmondsworth, Middlesex, England

First published 1968
Second edition 1978
5

Copyright © Ute Hitchin and Jill Norman, 1968, 1978
All rights reserved

Printed in England by Cox & Wyman Ltd, Reading, Berkshire

Contents

6 Contents

8 Contents

Introduction

In this series of phrase books only those words and phrases that are essential to the traveller have been included. For easy reference the phrases are divided into sections, each dealing with a different situation.

*Some of the German phrases are marked with an asterisk – these attempt to give an indication of the kind of reply you may get to your questions and of questions you may be asked.

At the end of the book is an extensive vocabulary list and here a pronunciation guide is given for each word. In addition there is an explanation of German pronunciation at the beginning of the book and a brief survey of the essential points of grammar. It would be advisable to read these sections before starting to use the book.

Pronunciation

The pronunciation guide is intended for people with no knowledge of German. As far as possible the system is based on English pronunciation. This means that complete accuracy may sometimes be lost for the sake of simplicity, but the reader should be able to understand German pronunciation, and make himself understood, if he reads this section carefully. In addition, each word in the vocabulary is given with a pronunciation guide. Stressed syllables are printed in **bold** type.

VOWELS

German vowels are much purer than English.

Long a	as 'a' in father	symbol ah	Abend – ahbent
Short a	as 'u' in mud	symbol u	kalt – cult
au	as 'ow' in how	symbol ow	Ausland – owslunt
ä	as 'ai' in air or 'e' in bed	symbol e	Gepäck – gepeck
äu	as 'oy' in boy	symbol oy	Gebäude – geboyder
Long e	as 'e' in they	symbol ay	gegen – gaygen
Short e	as 'e' in bed	symbol e	Bett – bet

e (final)	unlike English 'e' is pronounced at the end of a word, as 'er' in sister	symbol er	Tinte – tinter
	(NB 'er': in most cases the r is more pronounced than in English)	symbol air/er	Vater – fahtair Amerika – umaireekah über – uiber
eu	as 'oy' in boy	symbol oy	Feuer – foyer
ei	as 'i' in fine	symbol I	ein – ine leisten – listen
i	as 'i' in bit	symbol i	Schiff – shif
i	as 'ee' in weed	symbol ee	Familie – fumeelyer
ie	as 'ee' in meet	symbol ee	Bier – beer
Long o	as 'o' in nose	symbol oh	sofort – zohfort
Short o	as 'o' in not	symbol o	von – fon
o	as 'o' in order	symbol o	Nord – nort
ö	similar to sound in 'her' and 'first' but made with the lips well rounded	symbol er	schön – shern
u	as 'oo' in good	symbol ŏŏ	dunkel – dŏŏnkell
u	as 'oo' in mood	symbol ōō	Blut – blōōt
ü	similar to some Scottish pronunciations of 'u' in tone. Say 'i' as in bit with the lips rounded and pushed forward	symbol ui	Büro – buiroh

CONSONANTS

ch	rather like the sound of 'ch' in Scottish loch or the Welsh 'ch'	symbol kh	Buch – bōōkh
chs	as 'x' in six	symbol ks	Lachs – luks
d (final)	pronounced as 't'		Kind – kint
g	hard as 'g' in go, except in some endings		gut – gōōt
j	as 'y' in yacht	symbol y	ja – yah
kn	in German words which begin kn– the two sounds are pronounced separately, unlike English	symbol k-n	Knie – k-nee
qu	two sounds pronounced separately	symbol k-v	Qualität – k-vulit ayt
r	is always guttural and clearly pronounced.		
s	before a vowel is pronounced 'z' as in zoo	symbol z	Bluse – blōōzer
s	at the end of a word is pronounced 's' as in sale	symbol s/ss	Hals – huls das – duss
s	before p or t is pronounced 'sh' as in sheep	symbol sh	Stein – shtine Spiel – shpeel
sch	as 'sh' in sheep	symbol sh	Schuh – shōō
ss	often printed ß in German and pronounced as in English.		

th	as 't' in tent	symbol t	Theater – tayahtair
tz	as 'ts' in cuts	symbol ts	Netz – nets
v	as 'f' in foot or 'v' in vase	symbol f or v	viel – feel; vase – vahser
w	usually as 'v' in vase	symbol v	Wohnung – vohnōōng
x	as 'x' in wax	symbol cks	Taxi – tucksee
z	as 'ts' in bits	symbol ts	zu – tsōō

Basic grammar

There are four cases in German: NOMINATIVE (used for the subject or initiator of an action or speech), ACCUSATIVE (used for the person or thing directly affected by the action), DATIVE (used for the recipient), GENITIVE (used for the possessor). These cases are used for articles, nouns, pronouns and adjectives according to their position.

German also has three genders: masculine, feminine and neuter. They apply not only to living beings but also to inanimate objects: e.g. *der* Tisch (the table), *die* Tür (the door), *das* Bett (the bed). There are no clear rules for the use of the different genders. Similarly there are no precise easy rules on how to decline German nouns and these declensions have therefore been omitted.

DEFINITE ARTICLE

The definite article is declined as follows:

	Masculine	*Feminine*	*Neuter*	*Plural for all genders*	
Nom.	der	die	das	die	the
Acc.	den	die	das	die	the
Dat.	dem	der	dem	den	to the
Gen.	des	der	des	der	of the

The following words are declined in the same way as 'der, die, das':

Masculine	Feminine	Neuter	Plural for all genders	
dieser	diese	dieses	diese	this
jener	jene	jenes	jene	that
jeder	jede	jedes	jede	every, each
mancher	manche	manches	manche	many (a)
solcher	solche	solches	solche	such (a)
welcher?	welche?	welches?	welche?	which (one)?

INDEFINITE ARTICLE

The indefinite article is declined as follows:

	Masculine	Feminine	Neuter	
Nom.	ein	eine	ein	a
Acc.	einen	eine	ein	a
Dat.	einem	einer	einem	to a
Gen.	eines	einer	eines	of a

The following words are declined in the same way as 'ein, eine, ein' and, in addition, have a plural:

Masculine	Feminine	Neuter	Plural for all genders	
mein	meine	mein	meine	my
dein	deine	dein	deine	your
sein	seine	sein	seine	his, its
ihr	ihre	ihr	ihre	her, their
unser	uns(e)re	unser	uns(e)re	our
euer	eu(e)re	euer	eu(e)re	your
Ihr	Ihre	Ihr	Ihre	your
kein	keine	kein	keine	no, not a

Plural

Nom.	keine
Acc.	keine
Dat.	keinen
Gen.	keiner

Gen. keiner and, in the same way, the other words given above.

ADJECTIVES

The declension of adjectives is complex, but falls into a rigid pattern:

With the DEFINITE ARTICLE:

MASCULINE

	Singular		*Plural*
Nom.	der alte Mann	the old man	die alten Männer
Acc.	den alten Mann	the old man	die alten Männer
Dat.	dem alten Mann	to the old man	den alten Männern
Gen.	des alten Mannes	of the old man, the old man's	der alten Männer

FEMININE

	Singular		*Plural*
Nom.	die junge Frau	the young woman	die jungen Frauen
Acc.	die junge Frau	the young woman	die jungen Frauen
Dat.	der jungen Frau	to the young woman	den jungen Frauen
Gen.	der jungen Frau	of the young woman, the young woman's	der jungen Frauen

NEUTER

	Singular		*Plural*
Nom.	das kleine Kind	the small child	die kleinen Kinder
Acc.	das kleine Kind	the small child	die kleinen Kinder

Dat.	dem kleinen Kind	to the small child	den kleinen Kindern
Gen.	des kleinen Kindes	of the small child, the small child's	der kleinen Kinder

With the INDEFINITE ARTICLE:

MASCULINE

Nom.	ein alter Mann	an old man
Acc.	einen alten Mann	an old man
Dat.	einem alten Mann	to an old man
Gen.	eines alten Mannes	of an old man, an old man's

FEMININE

Nom.	eine junge Frau	a young woman
Acc.	eine junge Frau	a young woman
Dat.	einer jungen Frau	to a young woman
Gen.	einer jungen Frau	of a young woman, a young woman's

NEUTER

Nom.	ein kleines Kind	a small child
Acc.	ein kleines Kind	a small child
Dat.	einem kleinen Kind	to a small child
Gen.	eines kleinen Kindes	of a small child, a small child's

Without *either* article:

MASCULINE

	Singular		*Plural*
Nom.	süsser Wein	sweet wine	süsse Weine
Acc.	süssen Wein	sweet wine	süsse Weine
Dat.	süssem Wein	to sweet wine	süssen Weinen
Gen.	süssen Weines	of sweet wine	süsser Weine

FEMININE

	Singular		*Plural*
Nom.	alte Zeitung	old newspaper	alte Zeitungen
Acc.	alte Zeitung	old newspaper	alte Zeitungen
Dat.	alter Zeitung	to old newspaper	alten Zeitungen
Gen.	alter Zeitung	of old newspaper	alter Zeitungen

NEUTER

	Singular		*Plural*
Nom.	frisches Brot	fresh bread	frische Brote
Acc.	frisches Brot	fresh bread	frische Brote
Dat.	frischem Brot	to fresh bread	frischen Broten
Gen.	frischen Brot(e)s	of fresh bread	frischer Brote

PERSONAL PRONOUNS

Nominative		*Accusative*		*Dative*		*Genitive*	
ich	I	mich	me	mir	to me	meiner	mine
du	you	dich	you	dir	to you	deiner	yours
er	he	ihn	him	ihm	to him	seiner	his
sie	she	sie	her	ihr	to her	ihrer	hers
es	it	es	it	ihm	to it	seiner	its
wir	we	uns	us	uns	to us	unser	ours
ihr	you	euch	you	euch	to you	euer	yours
sie	they	sie	them	ihnen	to them	ihrer	theirs
Sie	you	Sie	you	Ihnen	to you	Ihrer	yours

'du' (singular) and 'ihr' (plural) are the familiar address used towards friends, relatives and children.

'Sie' (singular and plural) is the formal address used towards all other people. It is written with a capital 'S' when it means 'you' and small 's' when it means 'she', or 'they'.

PREPOSITIONS

The English meanings given in the list below are often only approximations, as prepositions in German are used to indicate a number of different meanings, e.g.

Ich wohne *bei* meinen Eltern = I am living *with* my parents.

Biegen Sie rechts *bei* den Verkehrsampeln ab = Turn right *at* the traffic lights.

With the *accusative* (i.e. they always govern the noun or pronoun in the accusative case):

durch	through
für	for
gegen	against
wider	against
ohne	without
um	round, at (of time)

With the *dative*:

mit	with
zu	to
nach	to (a place), after, according to
von	of, from, by
us	out of
bei	with, near, by
seit	since
gegenüber	opposite
ausser	except, besides

With the *accusative or dative*

in	in, into, inside
auf	on, onto

unter	under
über	over, above
an	at, on, against
vor	before, in front of
hinter	behind
zwischen	between
neben	near, beside

These prepositions are used with the *dative* when they indicate position or rest [e.g. Ich bin in dem Haus = I am in the house] or motion within a confined area [e.g. Ich gehe in dem Garten auf und ab = I am walking up and down in the garden]. They are used with the *accusative* if they indicate motion towards something or a change from one place to another [e.g. Ich gehe in das Haus = I go into the house].

With the *genitive*:

während	during
wegen	because of
trotz	in spite of
ausserhalb	outside
innerhalb	inside
statt/anstatt	instead of

INTERROGATIVE PRONOUNS

Nom.	wer?	who?	was?	what?
Acc.	wen?	whom?	was?	what?
Dat.	wem?	to whom?	wem?	to what?
Gen.	wessen?	whose?	wessen?	of what?

welcher? which? (see DEFINITE ARTICLE, p. 16)

NEGATIVES

nicht	not
nie, niemals	never

The position of these words in a sentence depends very much on the stress the speaker wants to put on them. Generally, however, they stand in front of the word or idea to be negated.

VERBS

In German, as in English, there are certain basic verbs that one uses over and over again. These are:

SEIN = to be

Present

ich bin	I am		
du bist	you are		
er		he	
sie } ist		she } is	
es		it	
wir sind	we are		
ihr seid	you are		
sie sind	they are		
Sie sind	you are		

Future

ich werde sein	I will be		
du wirst sein	you will be		
er		he	
sie } wird sein		she } will be	
es		it	
wir werden sein	we will be		
ihr werdet sein	you will be		
sie werden sein	they will be		
Sie werden sein	you will be		

Perfect

ich bin gewesen	I have been		
du bist gewesen	you have been		
er		he	
sie } ist gewesen		she } has been	
es		it	
wir sind gewesen	we have been		

Imperfect

ich war	I was		
du warst	you were		
er		he	
sie } war		she } was	
es		it	
wir waren	we were		

ihr seid gewesen	you have been	ihr wart	you were
sie sind gewesen	they have been	sie waren	they were
Sie sind gewesen	you have been	Sie waren	you were

HABEN = to have

Present

ich habe	I have
du hast	you have
er	he
sie } hat	she } has
es	it
wir haben	we have
ihr habt	you have
sie haben	they have
Sie haben	you have

Future

ich werde haben	I will have
du wirst haben	you will have
er	he
sie } wird haben	she } will have
es	it
wir werden haben	we will have
ihr werdet haben	you will have
sie werden haben	they will have
Sie werden haben	you will have

Perfect

ich habe gehabt	I have had
du hast gehabt	you have had
er	he
sie } hat gehabt	she } has had
es	it
wir haben gehabt	we have had
ihr habt gehabt	you have had
sie haben gehabt	they have had
Sie haben gehabt	you have had

Imperfect

ich hatte	I had
du hattest	you had
er	he
sie } hatte	she } had
es	it
wir hatten	we had
ihr hattet	you had
sie hatten	they had
Sie hatten	you had

Most German verbs are conjugated with 'haben' [e.g. Ich habe gesehen – I have seen]. The exceptions are the verb 'sein = to be' and all verbs of *motion* which are conjugated with 'sein' [e.g. Ich bin gelaufen – I have run, Ich bin gefahren – I have travelled].

AUXILIARY VERBS

These verbs are mostly used with the infinitive of another verb, and the latter always goes to the end of the sentence.

DÜRFEN = to be permitted (may)

Present	*Imperfect*
ich darf	ich durfte
du darfst	du durftest
er sie } darf es	er sie } durfte es
wir dürfen	wir durften
ihr dürft	ihr durftet
sie dürfen	sie durften
Sie dürfen	Sie durften

e.g. Darf ich rauchen? = May I smoke?

KÖNNEN = to be able to (can)

Present	*Imperfect*
ich kann	ich konnte
du kannst	du konntest
er sie } kann es	er sie } konnte es
wir können	wir konnten
ihr könnt	ihr konntet
sie können	sie konnten
Sie können	Sie konnten

e.g. Ich kann Sie nicht verstehen = I cannot understand you.

MÖGEN = to have the inclination, liking (combined with the probability)

Present	*Imperfect*
ich mag	ich mochte
du magst	du mochtest
er	er
sie } mag	sie } mochte
es	es
wir mögen	wir mochten
ihr mögt	ihr mochtet
sie mögen	sic mochten
Sie mögen	Sie mochten

e.g. Es mag richtig sein = It may well be right.
Ich mag diesen Tee nicht = I don't like this tea.

SOLLEN = to have to (shall) (under order)

Present	*Imperfect*
ich soll	ich sollte
du sollst	du solltest
er	er
sie } soll	sie } sollte
es	es
wir sollen	wir sollten
ihr sollt	ihr solltet
sie sollen	sie sollten
Sie sollen	Sie sollten

e.g. Er soll zu mir kommen = He shall come to me.

MÜSSEN = to have to (must)

Present	*Imperfect*
ich muss	ich musste
du musst	du musstest

er		er	
sie	muss	sie	musste
es		es	
wir müssen		wir mussten	
ihr müsst		ihr musstet	
sie müssen		sie mussten	
Sie müssen		Sie mussten	

e.g. Sie müssen um zehn Uhr hier sein = You have to be here at 10 o'clock.

WOLLEN = to want to, wish to (will)

Present		*Imperfect*	
ich will		ich wollte	
du willst		du wolltest	
er		er	
sie	will	sie	wollte
es		es	
wir wollen		wir wollten	
ihr wollt		ihr wolltet	
sie wollen		sie wollten	
Sie wollen		Sie wollten	

e.g. Ich will mit dem Zug fahren = I want to go by train.

WEAK VERBS

A large group of German verbs – known as 'weak' – are conjugated by changing their endings, for instance:

MACHEN = to make, do

Present		*Future*	
ich mache	I make	Ich werde machen	I will make
du machst	you make	du wirst machen	you will make

er	he		er	he	
sie } macht	she } makes		sie } wird machen	she } will make	
es	it		es	it	
wir machen	we make		wir werden machen	we will make	
ihr macht	you make		ihr werdet machen	you will make	
sie machen	they make		sie werden machen	they will make	
Sie machen	you make		Sie werden machen	you will make	

Imperfect

ich machte	I made
du machtest	you made

er	he
sie } machte	she } made
es	it

wir machten	we made
ihr machtet	you made
sie machten	they made
Sie machten	you made

Perfect

ich habe gemacht	I have made
du hast gemacht	you have made

er	he
sie } hat gemacht	she } has made
es	it

wir haben gemacht	we have made
ihr habt gemacht	you have made
sie haben gemacht	they have made
Sie haben gemacht	you have made

STRONG VERBS

However, many of the verbs in this phrase book can be grouped together as 'strong' verbs which means their form changes more drastically in different tenses.

SPRECHEN = to talk, speak

Present

ich spreche	I speak
du sprichst	you speak

Future

ich werde sprechen	I will speak
du wirst sprechen	you will speak

er	he		er	he
sie } spricht	she } speaks		sie } wird sprechen	she } will speak
es	it		es	it
wir sprechen	we speak		wir werden sprechen	we will speak
ihr sprecht	you speak		ihr werdet sprechen	you will speak
sie sprechen	they speak		sie werden sprechen	they will speak
Sie sprechen	you speak		Sie werden sprechen	you will speak

Imperfect

ich sprach	I spoke
du sprachst	you spoke
er	he
sie } sprach	she } spoke
es	it
wir sprachen	we spoke
ihr spracht	you spoke
sie sprachen	they spoke
Sie sprachen	you spoke

Perfect

ich habe gesprochen	I have spoken
du hast gesprochen	you have spoken
er	he
sie } hat gesprochen	she } has spoken
es	it
wir haben gesprochen	we have spoken
ihr habt gesprochen	you have spoken
sie haben gesprochen	they have spoken
Sie haben gesprochen	you have spoken

A list of the most common 'strong' verbs is given below:

Infinitive	3rd person singular present	Imperfect	Past participle	
beginnen	beginnt	begann	begonnen	to begin
biegen	biegt	bog	gebogen	to bend, turn
bitten	bittet	bat	gebeten	to entreat, beg (... um = ask for)
bleiben	bleibt	blieb	geblieben	to remain, stay
bringen	bringt	brachte	gebracht	to bring
denken	denkt	dachte	gedacht	to think
empfehlen	empfiehlt	empfahl	empfohlen	to recommend
essen	isst	ass	gegessen	to eat

fahren	fährt	fuhr	gefahren	to drive, travel
fangen	fängt	fing	gefangen	to catch
finden	findet	fand	gefunden	to find
fliegen	fliegt	flog	geflogen	to fly
geben	gibt	gab	gegeben	to give
gefallen	es gefällt (mir)	gefiel	gefallen	to like
gehen	geht	ging	gegangen	to go
geschehen	es geschieht	geschah	geschehen	to happen
halten	hält	hielt	gehalten	to hold
heissen	heisst	hiess	geheissen	to be called
helfen	hilft	half	geholfen	to help
kennen	kennt	kannte	gekannt	to know
kommen	kommt	kam	gekommen	to come
lassen	lässt	liess	gelassen	to leave, let
laufen	läuft	lief	gelaufen	to run
liegen	liegt	lag	gelegen	to lie
nehmen	nimmt	nahm	genommen	to take
rufen	ruft	rief	gerufen	to call
schliessen	schliesst	schloss	geschlossen	to close, shut
schreiben	schreibt	schrieb	geschrieben	to write
sehen	sieht	sah	gesehen	to see
sitzen	sitzt	sass	gesessen	to sit
sprechen	spricht	sprach	gesprochen	to speak, talk
stehen	steht	stand	gestanden	to stand
tragen	trägt	trug	getragen	to carry, wear
treffen	trifft	traf	getroffen	to meet
treten	tritt	trat	getreten	to step
trinken	trinkt	trank	getrunken	to drink
tun	tut	tat	getan	to do, make
vergessen	vergisst	vergass	vergessen	to forget
verlieren	verliert	verlor	verloren	to lose
verstehen	versteht	verstand	verstanden	to understand

| werden | wird | wurde | geworden | to become |
| wissen | weiss | wusste | gewusst | to know |

SEPARABLE VERBS

There are some verbs in German which, by having a prefix added, modify their meaning:

e.g. kommen — to come
    ankommen — to arrive

    fangen — to catch
    anfangen — to start

    fahren — to travel, drive
    abfahren — to depart

When conjugated the prefix is separated from the verb in the present and imperfect and put at the end of the sentence.

e.g. abfahren: Der Zug *fährt* bald *ab* = The train leaves soon.

Essentials &

First things

Yes	Ja
No	Nein
Please	Bitte
Thank you	Danke
You're welcome	Bitte sehr
No, thank you	Nein danke
Sorry	Verzeihung

Language problems

I'm English/American	Ich bin Engländer(in)/ Amerikaner(in)
Do you speak English?	Sprechen Sie Englisch?
Does anybody here speak English?	Spricht hier irgend jemand Englisch?
I don't speak (much) German	Ich spreche kein/nur wenig Deutsch
Do you understand (me)?	*Verstehen Sie (mich)?
I don't understand	Ich verstehe nicht*
Would you say that again, please?	Würden Sie das bitte noch einmal sagen?
Please speak slowly	Bitte, sprechen Sie langsam
What does that mean?	Was bedeutet das?
Can you translate this for me?	Können Sie das für mich übersetzen?
Please write it down	Bitte schreiben Sie es auf
What do you call this in German?	Wie heisst das auf Deutsch?
How do you say that in German?	Wie sagt man das auf Deutsch?

Questions

Where is/are . . . ?	Wo ist/sind . . . ?
When?	Wann?
How?	Wie?
How much is/are . . . ?	Wie teuer ist/sind . . . ?/Was kostet/kosten . . . ?
How far?	Wie weit?
What's that?	Was ist das?
Who is that?	Wer ist das?
What do you want?	Was wünschen Sie?
What must I do?	Was muss ich tun?
Why?	Warum?
Have you . . . ?	Haben Sie . . . ?
Is there . . . ?	Gibt es . . . ?
Have you seen . . . ?	Haben Sie . . . gesehen?
May I have . . . ?	Darf ich . . . haben?
I should like . . .	Ich möchte . . .
I want . . .	Ich will . . .
I don't want . . .	Ich will nicht . . .
What's the matter?	Was ist los?
Can I help you?	*Kann ich Ihnen helfen?
Can you help me?	Können Sie mir helfen?

Can you tell/give/show me?	Können Sie mir ... sagen/ geben/zeigen?

Useful statements

Here is/are ...	Hier ist/sind ...
I (don't) like it	Es gefällt mir (nicht)
I (don't) know	Ich weiss (nicht)
I didn't know that ...	Ich wusste nicht dass ...
I think so	Ich glaube
I'm hungry/thirsty	Ich habe Hunger/Durst
I'm tired/ready	Ich bin müde/fertig
I'm in a hurry	Ich habe es eilig
Leave me alone	Lassen Sie mich in Ruhe
Just a minute	Einen Augenblick
This way, please	Hier entlang bitte
Take a seat	Nehmen Sie Platz
Come in!	Herein!
It's cheap	Es ist billig
It's (too) expensive	Es ist (zu) teuer
That's all	Das ist alles
You're right	Sie haben recht
You're wrong	Das stimmt nicht

Greetings

Good morning	Guten Morgen
Good day/afternoon	Guten Tag
Good evening	Guten Abend
Good night	Gute Nacht
Goodbye	Auf Wiedersehen
How are you?	Wie geht es Ihnen?
Very well, thank you	Danke, gut
See you soon/tomorrow	Bis bald/morgen
Have a good journey	Gute Reise
Have a good time	Viel Vergnügen
Good luck/all the best	Viel Glück/alles Gute

Polite phrases

Sorry	Verzeihung
Excuse me	Entschuldigen Sie bitte
Everything all right?	Alles in Ordnung?
Can't complain	Ich kann mich nicht beklagen
Don't mention it/you're welcome	Bitte sehr
Don't worry	Machen Sie sich keine Sorgen

It's a pity	(Es ist) schade	
It doesn't matter	(Es) macht nichts	
I beg your pardon?	Wie bitte?	
Am I disturbing you?	Störe ich Sie?	
I'm sorry to have troubled you	Es tut mir leid, dass ich Sie belästigt habe	
Good/that's fine	Gut/das ist gut so	
Thanks for your trouble	Besten Dank für Ihre Mühe	

Opposites

before/after	vor/nach	for/nahkh
early/late	früh/spät	frui/shpayt
first/last	erste/letzte	airster/letster
now/later, then	jetzt/dann	yetst/dun
far/near	weit/nah	vite/nah
here/there	hier/dort	heer/dort
in/out	in/aus	in/ows
inside/outside	drinnen/draussen	drinnen/drowsen
under/over	unter/über	öontair/uibair
big, large/small	gross/klein	grohs/kline
deep/shallow	tief/seicht	teef/zikht

empty/full	leer/voll	layr/fol
fat/lean	fett, dick/mager	fet, dick/**mahgair**
heavy/light	schwer/leicht	shvair/līkht
high/low	hoch/niedrig	hohkh/needrikh
long, tall/short	lang/kurz	lung/kŏŏrts
narrow/wide	schmal/breit	shmahl/brīte
thick/thin	dick/dünn	dick/duin
least/most	mindest/meist	mindest/mīst
many/few	viel(e)/wenig(e)	feel/**vaynikh**
more/less	mehr/weniger	mair/**vaynigair**
much/little	viel/wenig	feel/**vaynikh**
beautiful/ugly	schön/hässlich	shern/**heslikh**
better/worse	besser/schlechter	besser/**shlekhter**
cheap/dear	billig/euer	billikh/toyer
clean/dirty	sauber/schmutzig	zowber/shmŏŏtsikh
cold/hot, warm	kalt/heiss, warm	cult/his, vurm
easy/difficult	leicht/schwierig	līkht/**shveerikh**
fresh/stale	frisch/schal, alt	frish/shahl, ult
good/bad	gut/schlecht	gŏŏt/shlekht
new, young/old	neu, jung/alt	noy, yŏŏng/ult
nice/nasty	nett/eklig	net/ayklikh
right/wrong	richtig/falsch	reekhtikh/fulsh

free/taken	frei/besetzt	fri/bezetst
open/closed, shut	offen/geschlossen	offen/geshlossen
quick/slow	schnell/langsam	shnel/lungzum
quiet/noisy	ruhig/laut	roo-ikh/lowt
sharp/blunt	scharf/stumpf	shurf/shtöömpf

Signs and public notices[1]

Achtung	caution
Aufzug	lift/elevator
Ausgang	exit
Auskunft	information
Ausverkauf	sale
Ausverkauft	sold out/house full
Bank	bank
Berühren verboten	do not touch
Besetzt	occupied/engaged
Bitte klingeln/klopfen	please ring/knock
Damen	ladies
Dolmetscher	interpreter
Drücken	push
Einbahnstrasse	one way street
Eingang	entrance

1. See also ROAD SIGNS (p. 61).

Eintritt frei	admission free
Es wird gebeten, nicht ...	you are requested not to ...
Frauen	women
Frei	free/vacant
(Fremden) führer	guide
Fussgänger	pedestrians
Gefahr	danger
Geöffnet von ... bis ...	open from ... to ...
Geschlossen	closed
Herren	gentlemen
Kasse	cash desk
Kein Eingang	no entry
Kein Trinkwasser	not for drinking
Keine Zimmer frei	no vacancies
Kein Zutritt	no entry
Männer	men
Nicht ...	do not ...
Nichtraucher	no smoking
Notausgang	emergency exit
Offen	open
Polizei	police
Post	post office
Privat	private
Rauchen verboten	no smoking

Rechts halten	keep right
Reserviert	reserved
Schlussverkauf	sale
Stehplätze	standing room
Toilette	lavatory/toilet
Trinkwasser	drinking water
Unbefugten ist das Betreten verboten	trespassers will be prosecuted
Vorsicht	caution
Warten	wait
Ziehen	pull
Zimmer frei	vacancies
Zimmer zu vermieten	room to let
Zoll	customs
Zutritt verboten	no admission

Abbreviations

ADAC	Allgemeiner Deutscher Automobil-Club	German Automobile Association
AG	Aktien-Gesellschaft	company
Bhf	Bahnhof	railway station
BRD	Bundesrepublik Deutschland	German Federal Republic

b.w.	bitte wenden	p.t.o.
DB	Deutsche Bundesbahn	German Railways
DDR	Deutsche Demokratische Republik	German Democratic Republic
d.h.	das heisst	i.e.
DIN	Deutsche Industrie-Norm	industrial standard (like B.S.)
DM	Deutschmark	German Mark
DSG	Deutsche Schlafwagen-Gesellschaft	German Sleeping Car Co.
EWG	Europäische Wirtschafts-Gemeinschaft	E.E.C.
Frl.	Fräulein	Miss
GmbH	Gesellschaft mit beschränkter Haftung	limited company
Hbf.	Hauptbahnhof	central (main) station
km	Kilometer	kilometre (8 km = 5 miles)
Lkw	Lastkraftwagen	lorry, truck
m	Meter	metre
M.E.Z.	Mitteleuropäische Zeit	Central European time
Min	Minute	minute
MWSt	Mehrwehrtsteuer	V.A.T.
nachm.	nachmittags	in the afternoon
n.Chr.	nach Christus	A.D.

ÖAMTC	Oesterreichischer Automobil- Motorrad- und Touring-Club	Austrian Automobile, Motorcycle and Touring Club
ÖBB	Oesterreichische Bundesbahnen	Austrian Federal Railways
Pf.	Pfennig	penny
Pkw	Personenkraftwagen	(private) car
Pl.	Platz	square
S-Bahn	Vorortsbahn	suburban line
SBB	Schweizerische Bundesbahnen	Swiss Federal Railways
St.	Stock	floor
Std.	Stunde	hour
Str.	Strasse	street
tägl.	täglich	daily
TCS	Touring-Club der Schweiz	Swiss Touring Club
U-Bahn	Untergrundbahn	underground
usw.	undsoweiter	etc.
v.Chr.	vor Christus	B.C.
vorm.	vormittags	in the morning
W.E.Z.	Westeuropäische Zeit	West European (Greenwich) time
z.B.	zum Beispiel	e.g.
z.Z.	zur Zeit	at present

Money[1]

Is there a bank/exchange bureau near here?	Gibt es eine Bank/Wechselstube hier in der Nähe?
Do you cash traveller's cheques?	Lösen Sie Reiseschecks ein?
Where can I cash traveller's cheques?	Wo kann ich Reiseschecks einlösen?
I want to change some English/ American money	Ich möchte englisches/ amerikanisches Geld einwechseln.
How much do I get for a pound/ dollar?	Wieviel bekomme ich für ein englisches Pfund/einen Dollar?
Can you give me some small change?	Können Sie mir etwas Kleingeld geben?
Will you take a personal cheque?	Nehmen Sie einen Barscheck?

1. In Germany banks are open Monday to Thursday 9 a.m. to 5 p.m., Friday 9 a.m. to 4 p.m., closed Saturday.

In Austria banks are open from 8 a.m. to 12.30 p.m. and from 2.30 p.m. to 4 p.m., closed all day Saturday.

In Switzerland they are open from 8 or 8.30 a.m. to 5 p.m., closed all day Saturday.

Do you have any identification?	*Können Sie sich ausweisen?
Do you have a banker's card?	*Haben Sie eine Eurokarte?
Sign here, please	*Unterschreiben Sie hier bitte
Go to the cashier	*Gehen Sie zur Kasse
What is the current rate of exchange?	Wie ist der Wechselkurs im Augenblick?

CURRENCY

Austria: 100 Gr(oschen) = 1 S(chilling)
Germany: 100 Pf(ennige) = 1 DM (Deutschmark)
Switzerland: 100 c(entimes) = 1 F(ranc)

Travel

On arrival

Passport control	*die Passkontrolle
Your passport, please	*Ihren Pass bitte
Are you together?	*Sind Sie zusammen?
I'm travelling alone	Ich reise allein
I'm travelling with my wife/a friend	Ich reise mit meiner Frau/einem Freund
I'm here on business/on holiday	Ich bin geschäftlich hier/auf Urlaub hier
What is your address in . . .?	*Wie ist Ihre Adresse in . . .?
How long are you staying here?	*Wie lange bleiben Sie hier?
How much money have you got?	*Wieviel Geld haben Sie bei sich?
I have . . . DM/pounds/dollars	Ich habe . . . Mark/Pfund/Dollar
Customs	*der Zoll
Nothing to declare	*Zollfreie Waren

Goods to declare	*Zollpflichtige Waren
Which is your luggage?	*Welches ist Ihr Gepäck?
Do you have any more luggage?	*Haben Sie noch mehr Gepäck?
This is (all) my luggage	Das ist (all) mein Gepäck
Have you anything to declare?	*Haben Sie etwas zu verzollen?
I have only my personal things in it	Ich habe nur persönliche Sachen darin
I have a carton of cigarettes and a bottle of gin/wine	Ich habe eine Stange Zigaretten und eine Flasche Gin/Wein
Open your bag, please	*Öffnen Sie Ihre Tasche bitte
May I go through?	Kann ich durchgehen?
Where is the information bureau, please?	Wo ist die Auskunft bitte?
Porter!	Gepäckträger!
Would you take these bags to a taxi/the bus	Bringen Sie bitte diese Taschen zu einem Taxi/zum Bus
What's the price for each piece of luggage?	Wieviel verlangen Sie für jedes Gepäckstück?
I shall take this myself	Ich nehme dies selbst
That's not mine	Das gehört mir nicht
How much do I owe you?	Wieviel schulde ich Ihnen?

Signs to look for at stations, etc.

Arrivals	Ankunft
Booking Office/Tickets	Fahrkarten(schalter)
Buses	Busse
Connections	Verbindungen
Departures	Abfahrt
Exchange	Wechselstube
Gentlemen	Herren/Männer
Information	Auskunft
Ladies Room	Damen/Frauen
Left Luggage	Gepäckaufbewahrung
Lost Property	Fundbüro
Luggage lockers	Schliessfächer
Main Lines	Hauptstrecken
Non-Smoker	Nichtraucher
Platform	Gleis, Bahnsteig
Refreshments/Snack bar	Erfrischungen/Imbisstube
Reservations	Platzkarten
Smoker	Raucher
Suburban Lines	S-Bahn/Vorortsbahn
Taxi rank	Taxistand
Underground	U-Bahn
Waiting Room	Warteraum

Buying a ticket

Where's the nearest travel agency/tourist office?	Wo ist das nächste Reisebüro/Verkehrsamt[1]?
Have you a timetable, please?	Haben Sie einen Fahrplan bitte?
What's the tourist return fare to . . .?	Wieviel kostet eine Touristen-Rückfahrkarte nach . . .?
How much is it first class to . . .?	Wieviel kostet es erster Klasse nach . . .?
A second class single to . . .	Einmal zweiter Klasse nach . . .
Single/one way	Einfach
A day return to . . .	Eine Tagesrückfahrkarte nach . . .
Is there a special rate for children?	Gibt es für Kinder Ermässigung?
How old is he/she?	*Wie alt ist er/sie?
How long is this ticket valid?	Wie lange ist diese Fahrkarte gültig?
A book of tickets, please	Ein Fahrscheinheft bitte
Is there a supplementary charge?	Muss man Zuschlag bezahlen?

1. Every German city has a VERKEHRSAMT. It gives information about entertainment and has a list of hotels and rooms, a HOTEL-UND ZIMMERNACHWEIS. It will recommend a hotel or guest-house, give you the price and the address, and direct you there. There is a small fee for this service.

By train and underground

RESERVATIONS AND INQUIRIES

Where's the railway station/ main station?	Wo ist der Bahnhof/ Hauptbahnhof?
Where is the ticket office?	Wo ist der Fahrkartenschalter?
Two seats on the ... to ...	Ich möchte zwei Plätze reservieren für den Zug um ... nach ...
I want to reserve a sleeper	Ich möchte einen Schlafwagenplatz reservieren
How much does a couchette cost?	Wieviel kostet ein Liegeplatz?
I want to register this luggage through to ...	Ich möchte dieses Gepäck als Reisegepäck nach ... aufgeben
Is it an express or a local train?[1]	Ist es ein Schnellzug oder ein Personenzug?[1]
Is there an earlier/later train?	Wann fährt der Zug davor/ danach?
Is there a restaurant car on the train?	Hat der Zug einen Speisewagen?

1. Triebwagen – railcar (used on short distances between smaller places). Personenzug – local train (stops at even the smallest station). Eilzug – stops only at bigger places (but no supplementary charge). D-Zug – stops only at main stations (supplementary charge). F-Zug – luxury train between large cities (supplementary charge). TEE – Trans-Europe-Express (first class only with special luxury features).

CHANGING

Is there a through train to . . .?	Fährt ein Zug durch nach . . .?
Do I have to change?	Muss ich umsteigen?
Where do I change?	Wo muss ich umsteigen?
When is there a connection to . . .?	Wann habe ich Anschluss nach . . .?

DEPARTURE

When does the train leave?	Wann fährt der Zug ab?
Which platform does the train to . . . leave from?	Von welchem Bahnsteig fährt der Zug nach . . . ab?
Is this the train for . . .?	Ist dies der Zug nach . . .?
Close the doors	*Türen schliessen

ARRIVAL

When does it get to . . .?	Wann kommt er in . . . an?
Does the train stop at . . .?	Hält der Zug auch in . . .?
How long do we stop here?	Wie lange halten wir hier?
Is the train late?	Hat der Zug Verspätung?
When does the train from . . . get in?	Wann fährt der Zug von . . . ein?
At which platform?	Auf welchem Bahnsteig?
The train from . . . is now arriving on platform . . .	*Der Zug von . . . hat Einfahrt auf Gleis . . .

ON THE TRAIN

We have reserved seats	Wir haben Plätze reserviert
Is this seat free?	Ist dieser Platz frei?
This seat is taken	Dieser Platz ist besetzt
Conductor	der Schaffner, die Schaffnerin
Your tickets please	*Ihre Fahrkarten bitte

By air

Where's the airline office?	Wo ist das Flugbüro?
I'd like to book two seats on the plane to . . .	Ich möchte zwei Plätze buchen für das Flugzeug nach . . .
Is there a flight to . . . ?	Gibt es einen Flug nach . . . ?
What is the flight number?	Wie ist die Flugnummer?
When does the plane leave/ arrive?	Wann startet/landet das Flugzeug?
When's the next plane?	Wann fliegt die nächste Maschine?
Is there a coach to the airport/ town?	Fährt ein Bus zum Flughafen/ in die Stadt?

When must I check in?	Wann muss ich mich melden?
Please cancel my reservation to . . .	Bitte machen Sie meine Flugreservierung nach . . . rückgängig
I'd like to change my reservation	Ich möchte meine Flugreservierung umbestellen

By boat

Is there a boat/(car) ferry from here to . . .?	Fährt ein Schiff/(Auto) Fähre von hier nach . . .?
How long does the boat take?	Wie lange dauert die Fahrt?
How often do the boats leave?	Wie oft fährt ein Schiff ab?
Does the boat call at . . .?	Legt das Schiff in . . . an?
When does the next boat leave?	Wann fährt das nächste Schiff ab?
Can I book a single berth cabin?	Kann ich eine Einzelkabine buchen?
How many berths are there in the cabin?	Wieviele Betten sind in der Kabine?
When must we go on board?	Wann müssen wir an Bord gehen?

When do we dock?	Wann legen wir an?
How long do we stay in port?	Wie lange bleiben wir im Hafen?

By bus, coach or tram

Where's the bus station?	Wo ist der Omnibus-Bahnhof?
Bus stop	*Bushaltestelle
Request stop	*Bedarfshaltestelle
When does the coach leave?	Wann fährt der Bus ab?
When does the coach get to . . .?	Wann kommt der Bus in . . . an?
What stops does it make?	Wo hält der Bus überall?
How long is the journey?	Wie lange dauert die Fahrt?
We want to take a coach tour round the sights	Wir möchten eine Stadtrundfahrt machen
Is there a sightseeing tour?	Gibt es eine Stadtrundfahrt?
What is the fare?	Was kostet es?
Does the bus/coach stop at our hotel?	Hält der Bus bei unserem Hotel?
Is there an excursion to . . . tomorrow?	Fährt morgen ein Sonderbus nach . . .?
When's the next bus? . . .	Wann fährt der nächste Bus?
How often do the buses run?	Wie oft fahren die Busse?
Has the last bus gone?	Ist der letzte Bus schon weg?

Does this bus go to the town centre/beach/station?	Fährt dieser Bus in die Stadtmitte/zum Strand/zum Bahnhof?
Do you go near . . .?	Fahren Sie in die Nähe von . . .?
Where can I get a bus to . . .?	Von wo fährt ein Bus nach . . .?
Which bus goes to . . .?	Welcher Bus fährt nach . . .?
I want to go to . . .	Ich möchte nach . . . fahren
Where do I get off?	Wo muss ich aussteigen?
The tram to . . . stops over there	*Die Strassenbahn nach . . . hält dort drüben
You must take a number . . .	*Sie müssen mit der . . . fahren
You get off at the next stop	*Sie müssen an der nächsten Haltestelle aussteigen
The trams run every ten minutes/every hour	*Die Strassenbahnen fahren alle zehn Minuten/jede Stunde

By taxi

Please get me a taxi	Rufen Sie mir bitte ein Taxi
Where can I find a taxi?	Wo kann ich ein Taxi bekommen?
Are you free?	Sind Sie frei?

Please take me to the Hamburg hotel/the station/this address

Bitte fahren Sie mich zum Hotel Hamburg/zum Bahnhof/zu dieser Adresse

Can you hurry, I'm late?

Können Sie sich bitte beeilen, ich habe mich verspätet

Please wait for me

Bitte warten Sie auf mich

Stop here

Halten Sie hier

Is it far?

Ist es weit?

How much do you charge by the hour/for the day?

Wieviel verlangen Sie pro Stunde/pro Tag?

How much will you charge to take me to . . .?

Wieviel verlangen Sie für die Fahrt nach . . .?

How much is it?

Wieviel muss ich zahlen?

That's too much

Das ist zu viel

Directions

Excuse me, could you tell me . . .	Entschuldigen Sie bitte, können Sie mir sagen . . .
Where is . . .?	Wo ist . . .?
How do I get to . . .?	Wie komme ich nach . . .?
How far is it to . . .?	Wie weit ist es nach . . .?
How many kilometres?	Wieviel Kilometer?
How do we get on to the motorway to . . .?	Wie kommen wir auf die Autobahn nach . . .?
Which is the best road to . . .?	Welches ist die beste Strasse nach . . .?
Is there a scenic route to . . .?	Gibt es eine Grüne Strasse nach . . .?
Where does this road lead to?	Wohin führt diese Strasse?
Is it a good road?	Ist die Strasse gut?
Is it a motorway?	Ist es eine Autobahn?
Is there any danger of snowdrifts?	Besteht Gefahr von Schneewehen?

Will we get to . . . by evening?	Werden wir bis zum Abend in . . . sein?
Where are we now?	Wo sind wir jetzt?
What is the name of this place?	Wie heisst dieser Ort?
Please show me on the map	Bitte, zeigen Sie mir auf der Karte
It's that way	*Da entlang
It isn't far	*Es ist nicht weit
Follow this road for five kilometres	*Fahren Sie auf dieser Strasse fünf Kilometer
Keep straight on	*Fahren Sie geradeaus
Turn right at the crossroads	*Biegen Sie bei der Kreuzung nach rechts ab
Take the second road on the left	*Biegen Sie in die zweite Strasse links ein
Turn right at the traffic-lights	*Biegen Sie bei der Verkehrsampeln rechts ab
Turn left after the bridge	*Biegen Sie hinter der Brücke links ab
The best road is the 35	*Am besten fahren Sie die 35
Take the 35 to . . . and ask again	*Fahren Sie auf der 35 bis . . . und fragen Sie dann wieder

Motoring

General

Have you a road map, please?

Haben Sie bitte eine Strassenkarte?

Where is the nearest car park/ garage?

Wo ist der nächste Parkplatz/ die nächste Garage?

(How long) can I park here?

(Wie lange) kann ich hier parken?

May I see your licence/logbook, please?

*Kann ich bitte Ihren Führerschein/ Kraftfahrzeugschein sehen?

Is this your car?

*Ist das Ihr Wagen/Auto?

How far is the next petrol station?

Wie weit ist es bis zur nächsten Tankstelle?

Car hire

Where can I hire a car?	Wo kann ich ein Auto mieten?
I want to hire a small/large car	Ich möchte einen kleinen/grossen Wagen mieten
I need it for two days/ a week	Ich brauche ihn für zwei Tage/eine Woche
How much is it by the hour/day/week?	Was kostet es pro Stunde/Tag/Woche?
Does that include mileage?	Ist Kilometergeld im Preis einbegriffen?
The charge per kilometre is . . .	*Die Gebühr pro Kilometer ist . . .
Do you want full insurance?	*Möchten Sie eine Vollkaskoversicherung?
What is the deposit?	Wieviel muss ich hinterlegen?
May I see your driving licence?	*Kann ich Ihren Führerschein sehen?
Would you sign here, please?	*Unterschreiben Sie hier, bitte
Can I return it in . . .?	Kann ich ihn in . . . zurückbringen?
Could you show me the controls/lights, please?	Können Sie mir bitte die Schaltung/Beleuchtung zeigen?

Road signs

Ausfahrt (für Lkws)	exit (for lorries)
Bahnübergang	level crossing
Blaue Zone	restricted parking
Durchgangsverkehr	through traffic
Einbahnstrasse	one-way street
Einordnen	get in lane
Gefahr	danger
Geschwindigkeitsgrenze	speed limit
Halt!	stop!
Keine Zufahrt	no entry
Kurven	bends, curves
Langsam (fahren)	(go) slow
Lawinengefahr	avalanche area
Licht einschalten	lights on
Nicht überholen	overtaking prohibited
Parken nur mit Parkscheiben	parking discs required
Parken verboten	no parking
Rechts fahren	keep right
Scheinwerfer einschalten	headlights on
Schlechte Fahrbahn	bad surface
Seitenstreifen nicht befahrbar	soft verges
Steinschlag	falling rock

Strasse gesperrt	road blocked
Strassenbau	roadworks ahead
Strassenglätte	slippery surface
Umleitung	diversion
Verkehrsampeln	traffic lights
Vorfahrt beachten	give way
Vorsicht	caution
Zoll	customs

At the garage or petrol station

Fill it up, please	(Füllen Sie den Tank) voll, bitte
How much is petrol a litre?	Wie teuer ist das Benzin pro Liter?
. . . litres of standard/premium petrol, please	. . . Liter Normal/Super, bitte
. . . pounds' worth of petrol, please	Für . . . Mark Benzin, bitte
Please check the oil and water	Bitte prüfen Sie das Öl und das Wasser
Could you check the brake/ transmission fluid, please?	Prüfen Sie bitte die Bremsflüssigkeit/ Getriebeflüssigkeit

Would you clean the windscreen, please?	Machen Sie bitte die Windschutzscheibe sauber
The oil needs changing	Das Öl muss gewechselt werden
Check the tyre pressures, please	Prüfen Sie bitte den Reifendruck
Please wash the car	Bitte waschen Sie den Wagen
Can I garage the car here?	Kann ich den Wagen hier einstellen?
What time does the garage close?	Wann wird die Garage geschlossen?
Where are the toilets?	Wo sind die Toiletten?

SELF-SERVICE PUMPS

Instructions on the pump:

1. Tankverschluss öffnen (take off petrol filler cap)

2. Münzen einwerfen (insert coins, at least 2 DM, at most 30 DM. Coins that can be used: 1 DM, 2 DM, 5 DM)

3. Zapfventil abheben (lift off nozzle)

4. Zapfen (pour in petrol)

5. Zapfventil einhängen (replace nozzle)

6. Quittung entnehmen (take out receipt)

7. Geldrückgabe (money returned, in case of fault)

Repairs, etc.

My car is broken down	Ich habe eine Autopanne
May I use your phone?	Darf ich Ihr Telefon benutzen?
Where is there a . . . agent?	Wo gibt es eine . . . Vertretung?
Have you a breakdown service?	Haben Sie einen Abschleppdienst?
Is there a mechanic?	Haben Sie einen Mechaniker?
Can you send someone to look at it/tow it away?	Können Sie jemanden schicken, der sich den Wagen ansieht/ der den Wagen abschleppt
It is an automatic and cannot be towed	Er hat ein automatisches Getriebe und kann nicht abgeschleppt werden
Where are you?	*Wo sind Sie?
Where is your car?	*Wo ist Ihr Wagen?
I am on the road from . . . to . . . near kilometre post . . .	Ich bin auf der Strasse von . . . nach . . . in der Nähe von Kilometerstein . . .
How long will you be?	Wie lange wird es dauern?
I want the car serviced	Ich möchte den Wagen überholen lassen
This tyre is flat, can you mend it?	Dieser Reifen ist platt, können Sie ihn reparieren?
The valve/radiator is leaking	Das Schlauchventil/der Kühler ist undicht

The battery is flat, it needs charging	Die Batterie ist leer, sie muss aufgeladen werden
My car won't start	Mein Wagen fährt nicht an
It's not running properly	Er läuft nicht richtig
The engine is overheating/firing badly	Der Motor läuft sich heiss/hat Fehlzündung
Can you change this faulty plug?	Können Sie diese Zündkerze auswechseln?
There's a petrol/oil leak	Ich verliere Benzin/Öl
There's a smell of petrol/rubber	Es riecht nach Benzin/Gummi
There's a rattle/squeak	Es klappert/quietscht
Something is wrong with my car/the engine/the lights/the clutch/the gearbox/the brakes/the steering	Etwas funktioniert nicht an meinem Wagen/an dem Motor/an dem Licht/an der Kupplung/am Getriebe/an der Bremse/an der Steuerung
I've got electrical/mechanical trouble	Der Wagen hat einen elektrischen/mechanischen Defekt
The carburettor needs adjusting	Der Vergaser muss eingestellt werden
I've lost my car key	Ich habe meinen Autoschlüssel verloren
Can you repair it?	Können Sie es reparieren?
How long will it take to repair?	Wie lange wird die Reparatur dauern?
What will it cost?	Wie teuer ist es?

When can I pick the car up?	Wann kann ich den Wagen abholen?
It will take two days	*Es dauert zwei Tage
We can repair it temporarily	*Wir können es vorübergehend reparieren
We haven't the right spares	*Wir haben nicht die richtigen Ersatzteile
We have to send for the spares	*Wir müssen uns die Ersatzteile schicken lassen
You will need a new ...	*Sie brauchen ein (eine, einen) neues (neue, neuen) ...
Could I have an itemized bill, please?	Geben Sie mir bitte eine Rechnung mit Einzelangaben

Parts of a car

accelerate (to)	beschleunigen	beshloynigen
accelerator	das Gaspedal	guspedahl
anti-freeze	der Frostschutz	frostshöōts
axle	die Achse	ugser
battery	die Batterie	butteree
bonnet	die Motorhaube	möhtorbowber
boot/trunk	der Gepäckraum	gepeckrowm
brake	die Bremse	bremser

brake lining	der Bremsbelag	bremsbelahg
breakdown	die Panne	punner
bulb	die Glühbirne	gluibeerner
bumper	die Stoss-stange	shtos-shtanger
carburettor	der Vergaser	fergahser
choke	die Drossel	drossel
clutch	die Kupplung	kōōplōōng
cylinder	der Zylinder	tseelinder
differential gear	das Ausgleichgetriebe	owsglikhgetreeber
dip stick	der Ölmesser	erlmesser
distilled water	das destillierte Wasser	destileerter vusser
distributor	der Verteiler	fertiler
door	die Tür	tuir
doorhandle	der Türgriff	tuirgrif
drive (to)	fahren	fahren
dynamo	der Dynamo	duinahmo
engine	der Motor	mohtor
exhaust	der Auspuff	owspōōf
fanbelt	der Ventilatorriemen	fenteelator-reemen
(oil) filter	der (Öl) Filter	erlfilter
foglamp	die Nebellampe	naybellumper
fusebox	die Sicherungsdose	zeekhairōōngsdohzer
gasket	der Dichtungsring	dikhtōōngsring
gears	die Gänge	gainger

gear-box	das Getriebe	getreeber
gear-lever	der Schalthebel	shulthaybel
grease (to)	schmieren	shmeeren
handbrake	die Handbremse	huntbremser
heater	die Heizung	hītsōŏng
horn	die Hupe	hōŏper
ignition	die Zündung	tsuindōŏng
ignition key	der Zündschlüssel	tsuindshluisel
indicator	der Winker	vinker
jack	der Wagenheber	vahgenhayber
lights – head/side/ rear	der Scheinwerfer/das Standlicht, Parklicht/das Schlusslicht	shīnevairfer/ shtuntlikht/ purklikht/ shlōŏslikht
lock/catch	das Schloss	shlos
mirror	der Spiegel	shpeegel
number plate	das Nummernschild	nōŏmernshilt
nut	die Mutter	mōŏter
oil	das Öl	erl
petrol	das Benzin	bentseen
petrol can	der Benzinkanister	bentseen-cunister
propeller shaft	die Gelenkwelle	gelenk-veller
piston	der Kolben	kolben
plug	die Zündkerze	tsuint-kairtser
points	die Kontakte	kontukter

(fuel/water) pump	die (Benzin/Wasser) Pumpe	pōōmper
puncture	die Reifenpanne	rīfenpunner
radiator	der Kühler	kuilair
reverse (to)	rückwärts fahren	ruikvairts fahren
reverse gear	der Rückwärtsgang	ruikvairtsgung
(sliding) roof	das (Schiebe) Dach	dukh
seat	der Sitz	zits
shock absorber	der Stossdämpfer	shtohsdaimpfer
silencer	der Auspufftopf	owspōōftopf
spares	die Ersatzteile	airsutstiler
(plug) spanner	der Schrauben- schlüssel	shrowbenshluisel
speed	die Geschwindigkeit	geshvindikh-kīte
speedometer	der Zähler	tsaylair
spring	die Feder	faydair
stall (to)	stehenbleiben	shtayen-blīben
starter	der Anlasser, Starter	unlusser, shturter
steering	die Steuerung	shtoyerōōng
steering wheel	das Steuerrad	shtoyer-raht
suspension	die Federung	fayderōōng
tank	der (Benzin) tank	tunk
tappets	die Stössel	shtersel
transmission	die Kraftübertragung	kruftuiber-trahgōōng

(spare) tyre	der (Ersatz) Reifen	(airsuts)rifen
valve	das Schlauchventil	shlowkh-fenteel
wheel	das Rad	raht
window	das Fenster	fenstair
windscreen	die Windschutz-scheibe	vintshŏŏts-shiber
windscreen washers	die Scheibenwasch-anlage	shiben-vushunlahger
windscreen wiper	der Scheibenwischer	shiben-vishair

Accommodation

Booking a room

Rooms to let/vacancies	*Zimmer zu vermieten/Zimmer frei
No vacancies	*Keine Zimmer frei
Have you a room for the night?	Haben Sie ein Zimmer für die Nacht?
Do you know another good hotel?	Kennen Sie ein anderes gutes Hotel?
I've reserved a room; my name is . . .	Ich habe ein Zimmer reserviert; mein Name ist . . .
I want a single room with a shower	Ich möchte ein Einzelzimmer mit Dusche
I want a room with a double bed and a bathroom	Ich möchte ein Doppelzimmer mit Bad
Have you a room with twin beds?	Haben Sie ein Zweibettzimmer?

How long will you be staying?	*Wie lange bleiben Sie?
Is it for one night only?	*Ist es nur für eine Nacht?
I want a room for two or three days/for a week/until Friday	Ich möchte ein Zimmer für zwei oder drei Tage/für eine Woche/bis Freitag
What floor is the room on?	In welchem Stock ist das Zimmer?
Is there a lift/elevator?	Gibt es einen Fahrstuhl?
Have you a room on the first floor?	Haben Sie ein Zimmer im ersten Stock?
May I see the room?	Kann ich bitte das Zimmer sehen?
I'll take this room	Ich nehme dieses Zimmer
I don't like this room	Dieses Zimmer gefällt mir nicht
Have you another one?	Haben Sie ein anderes?
I want a quiet room	Ich möchte ein ruhiges Zimmer
There's too much noise	Hier ist zu viel Lärm
I'd like a room with a balcony	Ich möchte ein Zimmer mit Balkon
Have you a room looking on to the street?	Haben Sie ein Zimmer zur Strassenseite?
Have you a room looking on to the sea?	Haben Sie ein Zimmer mit Blick auf das Meer?
Is there a telephone/radio/television in the room?	Hat das Zimmer Telefon/Radio/Fernsehen?

We've only a double/twin-bedded room	*Wir haben nur ein Doppelzimmer/Zweibettzimmer
This is the only room vacant	*Dies ist das einzige freie Zimmer
We shall have another room tomorrow	*Morgen wird ein anderes Zimmer frei
The room is only available tonight	*Das Zimmer ist nur für heute Nacht frei
How much is the room per night?	Wieviel kostet das Zimmer pro Nacht?
Have you nothing cheaper?	Haben Sie nichts Billigeres?
What do we pay for the child(ren)?	Was müssen wir für das Kind (die Kinder) bezahlen?
Could you put a cot in the room?	Könnten Sie ein Kinderbett ins Zimmer stellen?
Is the service (and tax[1]) included?	Ist Bedienung (und Kurtaxe) einbegriffen?
Are meals included?	Sind die Mahlzeiten einbegriffen?
How much is the room without meals?	Wieviel kostet das Zimmer ohne Mahlzeiten?
How much is the room with full board/with breakfast only?	Wieviel kostet das Zimmer mit Vollpension/nur mit Frühstück?
Do you do bed and breakfast?	Haben Sie Zimmer mit Frühstück?
Do you have a weekly rate?	Haben Sie einen festen Preis pro Woche?

1. In health resorts only.

Would you fill in the registration form, please? / *Füllen Sie bitte dieses Anmeldeformular aus

Could I have your passport, please? / *Könnte ich bitte Ihren Pass haben?

In your room

Room service / die Zimmerbedienung

I'd like breakfast in my room, please / Ich möchte bitte Frühstück in meinem Zimmer haben

There's no ashtray in my room / In meinem Zimmer ist kein Aschenbecher

Can I have more hangers, please? / Kann ich bitte mehr Kleiderbügel haben?

Is there a point for an electric razor? / Gibt es eine Steckdose für Rasierapparate?

What's the voltage? / Wie hoch ist die Spannung?

Where is the bathroom? / Wo ist das Badezimmer?

Where is the lavatory? / Wo ist die Toilette?

Is there a shower? / Gibt es eine Dusche?

There are no towels in my room / In meinem Zimmer sind keine Handtücher

There's no soap / Es gibt keine Seife

There's no (hot) water / Es gibt kein (heisses) Wasser

There's no plug in my washbasin	In meinem Waschbecken ist kein Stöpsel
There's no toilet paper in the lavatory	In der Toilette ist kein Papier
The lavatory won't flush	Die Spülung in der Toilette funktioniert nicht
May I have the key to the bathroom, please	Kann ich bitte den Schlüssel fürs Badezimmer haben?
May I have another blanket and sheet?	Kann ich bitte noch eine Wolldecke und ein Bettlaken haben?
May I have another pillow?	Kann ich bitte noch ein Kopfkissen haben?
I can't sleep under a continental quilt	Ich kann nicht unter einem Federbett schlafen
This sheet is dirty	Dieses Bettlaken ist schmutzig
I can't open my window, please open it	Ich kann mein Fenster nicht aufmachen, bitte öffnen Sie es für mich
It's too hot/cold	Es ist zu heiss/kalt
Can the heating be turned up?	Kann die Heizung weiter aufgedreht werden?
Can the heating be turned down?	Kann die Heizung etwas mehr abgedreht werden?
Is the room air-conditioned?	Hat das Zimmer Klima-anlage?
The air conditioning doesn't work	Die Klima-anlage funktioniert nicht

Come in	Herein
Put it on the table, please	Stellen Sie es bitte auf den Tisch
I want these shoes cleaned	Lassen Sie bitte diese Schuhe putzen
I want this dress cleaned	Lassen Sie bitte dieses Kleid reinigen
I want this suit pressed	Lassen Sie bitte diesen Anzug bügeln
When will it be ready?	Wann wird er fertig sein?
It will be ready tomorrow	*Es wird morgen fertig sein

At the porter's desk

My key, please	Meinen Schlüssel bitte
Have you a map of the town/an amusement guide?	Haben Sie einen Stadtplan/ein Veranstaltungsprogramm?
Can I leave this in your safe?	Könnten Sie dies in Ihren Tresor (Safe) legen?
Are there any letters for me?	Sind Briefe für mich da?
Is there any message for me?	Ist eine Nachricht für mich da?
If anyone phones, tell them I'll be back at 6.30	Wenn jemand anruft, sagen Sie bitte, ich bin um halb sechs wieder zurück

No one telephoned	*Es hat niemand angerufen
There's a lady/gentleman to see you	*Eine Dame/ein Herr möchte Sie sprechen
Please ask her/him to come up	Bitten Sie sie/ihn heraufzukommen
I'm coming down	Ich komme hinunter
Have you any writing paper/ envelopes/stamps?	Haben Sie Papier/ Umschläge/Briefmarken?
Please send the chambermaid/ the waiter	Schicken Sie mir bitte das Zimmermädchen/den Kellner
I need a guide/an interpreter	Ich brauche einen Fremdenführer/einen Dolmetscher
Where is the dining room?	Wo ist der Speisesaal?
What time is breakfast/lunch/ dinner?	Wann wird das Frühstück/das Mittagessen/das Abendessen serviert?
Is there a garage?	Gibt es eine Garage?
Is the hotel open all night?	Ist das Hotel die ganze Nacht offen?
What time does it close?	Wann wird es abgeschlossen?
Please wake me at . . .	Bitte wecken Sie mich um . . .

Departure

I want to leave tomorrow	Ich möchte morgen abfahren
Can we check out at . . .?	Können wir um . . . abfahren?
Can you have my bill ready?	Können Sie bitte meine Rechnung fertig machen?
I shall be coming back on . . ., can I book a room for that date?	Ich komme am . . . zurück, kann ich für die Zeit ein Zimmer reservieren?
Could you have my luggage brought down?	Können Sie bitte mein Gepäck runterbringen lassen?
Please order a taxi for me	Bitte bestellen Sie mir ein Taxi
Thank you for a pleasant stay	Vielen Dank für den angenehmen Aufenthalt

Meeting people

How are you/things?	Wie geht es Ihnen?/Wie steht's?
Fine, thanks, and you?	Gut, danke, und Ihnen?
May I introduce myself?	Darf ich mich vorstellen?
My name is ...	Mein Name ist ...
This is ...	Dies ist ...
Have you met ...?	Kennen Sie ...?
Glad to meet you	Es freut mich, Sie kennenzulernen/(*more emphatic*) Angenehm
What lovely/awful weather!	Was für ein schönes/scheussliches Wetter!
Isn't it cold/hot today?	Es ist kalt/warm heute, nicht wahr?
Do you think it's going to rain/snow?	Meinen Sie, wir werden Regen/Schnee bekommen?

Will it be sunny tomorrow?	Ob morgen wohl die Sonne scheinen wird?
Am I disturbing you?	Störe ich Sie?
Go away	Gehen Sie weg
Leave me alone	Lassen Sie mich in Ruhe
Sorry to have troubled you	Entschuldigen Sie die Störung
Do you live/are you staying here?	Wohnen Sie hier?
Is this your first time here?	Sind Sie zum erstenmal hier?
Do you like it here?	Gefällt es Ihnen hier?
Are you on your own?	Sind Sie allein(e)?
I am with my family/parents/a friend	Ich bin mit meiner Familie/ meinen Eltern/einem Freund (einer Freundin) hier
Where do you come from?	Woher sind Sie?
I come from ...	Ich komme aus ...
What do you do?	Was machen Sie beruflich?
What are you studying?	Was studieren Sie?
I'm on holiday/a business trip	Ich bin auf Urlaub/ geschäftlich hier
Would you like a cigarette?	Möchten Sie eine Zigarette?
Try one of mine	Probieren Sie eine von meinen
They're very mild/rather strong	Sie sind sehr milde/ziemlich stark

Do you have a light, please?	Haben Sie Feuer, bitte?
Do you smoke?	Rauchen Sie?
No, I don't, thanks	Nein, ich rauche nicht, danke
I have given it up	Ich habe es aufgegeben
Help yourself	Bedienen Sie sich
Can I get you a drink/another drink?	Kann ich Ihnen etwas zu trinken/noch etwas zu trinken holen?
I'd like . . . please	Ich hätte gern . . .
No thanks, I'm all right	Nein danke, ich möchte nichts

Going out

Are you waiting for someone?	Warten Sie auf jemanden?
Are you doing anything tonight/ tomorrow afternoon?	Haben Sie heute Abend/ morgen Nachmittag etwas vor?
Could we have coffee/a drink somewhere?	Können wir irgendwo einen Kaffee trinken/etwas trinken?
Would you go out with me?	Würden Sie mit mir ausgehen?
Shall we go to the cinema/ theatre	Sollen wir ins Kino/Theater gehen?
Shall we go to the beach?	Wollen wir an den Strand fahren?
Would you like to go dancing/ for a drive?	Möchten Sie tanzen gehen/ ausfahren?

Do you know a good disco/ restaurant?	Kennen Sie eine gute Diskothek/ ein gutes Restaurant?
Can you come to dinner/for a drink?	Können Sie zum Abendessen/ auf ein Gläschen zu uns kommen?
We're giving/There is a party. Would you like to come?	Wir geben/Es gibt eine Party. Möchten Sie auch kommen?
Can I bring a (girl) friend?	Kann ich einen Freund (eine Freundin) mitbringen?
Thanks for the invitation	Vielen Dank für die Einladung
Where shall we meet?	Wo sollen wir uns treffen?
What time shall I/we come?	Wann soll ich/sollen wir kommen?
I could pick you up at (*time/ place*)	Ich könnte Sie um ... von ... abholen
Could you meet me at (*time*) outside (*place*)?	Könnten wir uns um ... vor ... treffen?
What time do you have to be back?	Wann müssen Sie wieder zurück sein?
May I see you home?	Darf ich Sie nach Hause begleiten?
Can we give you a lift home/to your hotel?	Können wir Sie nach Hause/zu Ihrem Hotel fahren?
Can I see you again?	Können wir uns wiedersehen?
Where do you live?	Wo wohnen Sie?

What is your telephone number?	Wie ist Ihre Telefonnummer?
Do you live alone?	Wohnen Sie allein(e)?
Thanks for the evening/nice time	Vielen Dank für den netten Abend/die netten Stunden
It was lovely	Es war sehr nett
Hope to see you again soon	Hoffentlich sehen wir uns bald wieder
See you soon/later/tomorrow	Bis bald/später/morgen

Restaurant

Going to a restaurant

Can you suggest a good restaurant/a cheap restaurant/a vegetarian restaurant?	Können Sie ein gutes Restaurant/ein billiges Restaurant/ein vegetarisches Restaurant vorschlagen?
I'd like to book a table for four at 1 p.m.	Ich möchte einen Tisch für vier Personen für ein Uhr bestellen
I've reserved a table; my name is . . .	Ich habe einen Tisch reserviert; mein Name ist . . .
We did not make a reservation	Wir haben keinen Tisch reserviert
Have you a table for three?	Haben Sie einen Tisch für drei Personen?
Is there a table on the terrace/by the window/in a corner?	Haben Sie einen Tisch auf der Terrasse/beim Fenster/in der Ecke?
This way, please	*Hier entlang bitte

We shall have a table free in half an hour	*In einer halben Stunde haben wir einen Tisch frei
We don't serve lunch until 12.30	*Das Mittagessen wird erst um halb eins serviert
We don't serve dinner until 8 p.m.	*Das Abendessen wird erst um acht Uhr serviert
We stop serving at 9 o'clock	*Wir servieren nur bis neun Uhr
Where is the cloakroom?	Wo ist die Toilette?
It is downstairs	*Die Toiletten sind unten

Ordering

Service charge	*Bedienungsgeld
Service and V.A.T. not included	*Bedienung und Mehrwehrtsteuer nicht einbegriffen
Service and V.A.T. included	*(Unsere Preise sind) Endpreise
Cover charge	*Gedeck
Waiter/waitress (*address*)	Ober/Fräulein
May I see the menu/the wine list, please?	Darf ich bitte die Speisekarte/ die Weinkarte sehen?
Is there a set menu?	Gibt es ein Tagesgedeck?
I want something light	Ich möchte eine leichte Kost
We are in a hurry	Wir haben es eilig
Do you serve snacks?	Servieren Sie einen Imbiss?

Do you have children's helpings?	Haben Sie Kinderportionen?
What is your dish of the day?	Was ist Ihre Tagesspezialität?
What do you recommend?	Was empfehlen Sie?
Can you tell me what this is?	Können Sie mir sagen, was dies ist?
What is the speciality of the restaurant/of the region?	Was ist die Spezialität dieses Restaurants/dieser Gegend?
Would you like to try ...?	*Möchten Sie ... probieren?
There's no more ...	*... sind (ist) nicht mehr da
I'd like ...	Ich möchte ...
May I have peas instead of beans?	Darf ich Erbsen statt Bohnen haben?
Is it hot or cold?	Ist es warm oder kalt?
Where are our drinks?	Wo sind unsere Getränke?
Why is the food taking so long?	Warum müssen wir so lange auf unser Essen warten?
This isn't what I ordered, I want ...	Das habe ich nicht bestellt, ich möchte ...
Without sauce/oil, please	Ohne Sauce/Öl bitte
Some more bread, please	Noch etwas Brot bitte
A little more ...	Etwas mehr ...
This is bad	Dies ist schlecht
This is uncooked/overcooked	Dies ist nicht gar/zu lange gekocht
This is stale	Dies ist alt/schal

This is too cold/salty

Dies ist zu kalt/salzig

This plate/knife/spoon/glass is not clean

Dieser Teller/dieses Messer/ dieser Löffel/dieses Glas ist nicht sauber

Paying

The bill, please

Die Rechnung bitte/Ich möchte zahlen

Does it include service?

Ist Bedienung einbegriffen?

Please check the bill; I don't think it's correct

Bitte prüfen Sie die Rechnung; ich glaube, sie stimmt nicht

What is this amount for?

Wofür ist dieser Betrag?

I didn't have soup

Ich habe keine Suppe gehabt

I had chicken not beef

Ich hatte Huhn, nicht Rindfleisch

May we have separate bills?

Können wir bitte getrennte Rechnungen haben?

Do you take credit cards/ travellers' cheques?

Nehmen Sie Kreditkarten/ Reisechecks?

Keep the change

Das ist gut so

Breakfast and tea[1]

Breakfast	Das Frühstück
A white coffee, please	Eine Tasse Milchkaffee bitte
Black coffee (with cream)	Schwarzen Kaffee (mit Sahne)
A cup of tea, please	Eine Tasse Tee bitte
I would like tea with milk/lemon	Ich möchte Tee mit Milch/mit Zitrone
May we have some sugar, please?	Können wir bitte etwas Zucker haben?
A roll and butter, please	Ein Brötchen und Butter bitte
Toast	Toast
More butter, please	Etwas mehr Butter bitte
Have you some marmalade/jam/honey?	Haben Sie Orangenmarmelade/Marmelade/Honig?
I would like a (soft/hard) boiled egg	Ich möchte ein (weich/hart) gekochtes Ei
Ham	der Schinken
Cheese	der Käse
What fruit juices have you?	Was für Obstsäfte haben Sie?
Orange/tomato/(black, red) currant juice	der Apfelsinensaft (Orangensaft)/Tomatensaft/Johannisbeersaft (schwarz, rot)

1. Don't forget to go into a 'Cafe' or 'Konditorei', particularly in Austria. To try one of the wide selection of 'Torten', a pastry speciality, with names like Sachertorte, Kaffeecremetorte, Linzertorte, Imperialtorte, will be an experience for any foreign visitor.

Yoghurt	der Joghurt
Pastry[1]	das Gebäck
Flaky/short pastry	der Blätterteig/Mürbeteig
Tart/Layer cake	die Torte
Cake	der Kuchen

Snacks and picnics

Can I have a sandwich, please?	Kann ich bitte ein belegtes Brot haben?
What are those things over there?	Was ist das dort?
What are they made of?	Woraus ist es gemacht?
What is in them?	Was ist da drin?
I'll have one of these, please	Eins davon bitte
Beefburger	die Frikadelle
Biscuits	die Kekse
Bread	das Brot
Butter	die Butter
Cheese	der Käse
Chips	die Pommes frites
Chocolate bar	die Tafel Schokolade

1. For names of cakes and pastry see pp. 103–5.

Egg(s)	das Ei (die Eier)
Ham	der Schinken
Ice cream (*flavours: page* 103)	das Eis
Pancakes	der Pfannkuchen, die Palatschinke
Pickles	die Essigfrüchte
Meat/fruit pie	die Fleischpastete/Fruchttorte
Roll	das Brötchen
Salad	der Salat
Sausage (roll)	die Wurst(pastete)
Snack	der Imbiss
Snack bar	der Schnellimbiss
Soup	die Suppe
Tomato	die Tomate
Waffles	die Waffel

Drinks[1]

Bar	die Bar, die Schenke, der Ausschank
Café	das Café, das Kaffeehaus
What will you have to drink?	Was möchten Sie trinken?

1. For the names of beverages see pp. 106-8.

A bottle of the local wine, please	Eine Flasche hiesigen Wein bitte
I want to see the wine list	Ich möchte die Weinkarte sehen
Do you serve wine by the glass?	Haben Sie offenen Wein?
Carafe/glass	die Karaffe/das Glas[1]
Bottle/half bottle	die Flasche/kleine Flasche
Two glasses of beer, please	Zwei Gläser Bier bitte
Pint/half pint	ein grosses/kleines Bier
Do you have draught beer?	Haben Sie Bier vom Fass?
Light/dark beer	Helles/dunkles Bier
Two more beers	Noch zwei Bier
Neat/on the rocks	Pur/mit Eis
With (soda) water	mit (Soda) Wasser
Mineral water (with/without gas)	Mineralwasser (mit/ohne Kohlensäure)
Ice cubes	die Eiswürfel
Cheers!	Prost!
I'd like a glass of water, please	Ich möchte bitte ein Glas Wasser
The same again, please	Noch einmal dasselbe bitte
Three black coffees and one with cream	Dreimal schwarzen Kaffee und einen mit Sahne
Tea with milk/lemon	Tee mit Milch/Zitrone

1. Usually open wine is sold by the 'Viertel', a glass holding a quarter litre i.e. a third of a standard bottle or two of our standard glasses.

May we have an ashtray?

Können wir einen Aschenbecher haben?

Restaurant vocabulary

ashtray	der Aschenbecher	ushen-bekher
bill	die Rechnung	rekhnŏŏng
bowl	die Schüssel	shuisel
bread	das Brot	broht
butter	die Butter	bŏŏter
cigarettes	die Zigaretten	tseeguretten
cloakroom	die Toilette	twuletter
course (dish)	der Gang	gung
cream	die Sahne	zahner
cup	die Tasse	tusser
dressing	die Salatsosse	zulaht-sohser
fork	die Gabel	gahbel
glass	das Glas	glus
headwaiter	der Oberkellner	ohberkelnair
hungry (to be)	Hunger haben, hungrig sein	hŏŏngair hahben, hŏŏngrikh zine
knife	das Messer	messer
light (easily digested) meals	die Schonkost	shohnkost

matches	die Streichhölzer	shtrīkh-herltser
menu	die Speisekarte	shpīzerkurter
mustard	der Senf	zenf
napkin	die Serviette	zairveeyetter
oil	das Öl	erl
pepper	der Pfeffer	pfeffer
pickles	die Essigfrüchte	esikhfruikhter
plate	der Teller	tellair
restaurant	das Restaurant	restorunt
salt	das Salz	sults
sauce	die Sauce	sohser
saucer	die Untertasse	ōōntair-tasser
service	die Bedienung	bedeenōōng
spoon	der Löffel	lerffel
sugar	der Zucker	tsōōker
table	der Tisch	tish
tablecloth	das Tischtuch	tishtōōkh
thirsty (to be)	Durst haben, durstig sein	dōōrst hahben, dōōrstikh zine
tip	das Trinkgeld	trinkgelt
toothpick	der Zahnstocher	tsahn-shtokhair
vegetarian	der Vegetarier	fegetahree-er
vinegar	der Essig	essikh
waiter	der Kellner	kelnair

waitress	die Kellnerin	kelnairin
water	das Wasser	vussair

The menu

VORSPEISEN	HORS D'ŒUVRES
Artischocken	artichokes
Austern	oysters
Gänseleberpastete	pâté de foie
Geräucherter Lachs	smoked salmon
Königinpastete	pastry filled with *ragoût fin*
Matjesfilet ('Hausfrauenart')	herring fillet (with apple and sour cream)
(Geeiste) Melone	(iced) melon
Ölsardinen (mit Brot)	tinned sardines (with bread)
Räucheraal	smoked eel
Rollmops	rollmops
Russische Eier	hard boiled eggs with caviare, capers and mayonnaise
(Westfälischer) Schinken	(raw) ham
Schinkenwurst ⤫	ham sausage
(Weinberg)schnecken	snails
Spargelspitzen	asparagus tips

Stangenspargel mit Kräutersauce	asparagus with herb sauce
Strammer Max	ryebread, raw ham and fried egg
Wurstplatte	assorted sliced sausage

SUPPEN	SOUPS
Aalsuppe	eel soup
Bohnensuppe	bean soup
Erbsensuppe	pea soup
Gaisburger Marsch	vegetable soup with dumplings
Gemüsesuppe	vegetable soup (minestrone)
Gulaschsuppe	beef and paprika soup
Hühnerbrühe	chicken broth
Kartoffelsuppe	potato soup
Kirschkaltschale	cold cherry soup
Kraftbrühe mit Ei/Magen	bouillon with egg/tripe
Leberknödelsuppe	clear soup with liver dumplings
Linsensuppe	lentil soup
Mandelsuppe	almond and cream soup
Nudelsuppe	noodle soup
Ochsenschwanzsuppe	oxtail soup
Schildkrötensuppe	turtle soup
Tomatensuppe	tomato soup

Zwiebelsuppe	onion soup

FISCH	FISH
Aal	eel
Aal grün mit Dillsauce	fresh eel with dill sauce
Austern	oysters
Barsch	perch
Forelle	trout
Garnele	shrimp
Hecht	pike
Heilbutt	halibut
Hering	herring
Hummer	lobster
Kabeljau	cod
Karpfen	carp
Krabben	small shrimps
Krebs	crab
Lachs, Salm	salmon
Makrele	mackerel
Muscheln	mussels
Rotbarsch	redfish
Sardellen	anchovies
Schellfisch	haddock
Scholle	plaice

Seebarsch	bass
Seezunge	sole
Steinbutt	turbot
Thunfisch	tunny
Zander	pike-perch

FLEISCH

MEAT

Lamm/Hammel:
    Hammelbraten/Lammbraten
    Lammskeule
    Hammelragout

lamb/mutton:
    roast mutton/lamb
    roast leg of lamb
    mutton stew

Kalb:
    Kalbsbrust
    Kalbshaxe
    Kalbskoteletts
    Kalbsvögel
    (Wiener) Schnitzel

veal:
    breast of veal
    roast knuckle of veal
    veal cutlets, chops
    veal roulade
    (fried) escalope of veal

Rind:
    Beefsteak
    Deutsches Beefsteak
    gekochte Rinderbrust
    Gulasch
    Rinderbraten
    Rinderfilet
    Rindsrouladen
    Rinderschmorbraten
    Sauerbraten
    Stroganoff

beef:
    steak
    minced beef, hamburger
    boiled brisket of beef
    goulash
    roast beef
    fillet of beef
    stuffed beef
    braised beef
    braised pickled beef
    goulash of choice meat

Schweinefleisch:	pork:
(Kasseler) Rippchen	(smoked) pork chop
Schweinebraten	roast pork
Schweinefilet	loin of pork
Eisbein	pickled pork knuckle
Spanferkel	sucking pig

WÜRSTE UND INNEREIEN	SAUSAGES AND OFFAL
Blutwurst	black pudding
Bratwurst	frying sausage
Knackwurst	frankfurter
Kochwurst	cold cuts
Nürnberger Würstchen	small spiced chipolatas
Pinkel	smoked sausage with onions
Weisswurst	veal sausage
Flecke	tripe
Fleischkloss	meatball
Frikadelle	rissole, croquette
Hirn	brain
Kalbsbries (*North German:* Kalbsmilcher)	sweetbreads
Leber	liver
Nieren	kidneys
Ochsenschwanz	oxtail

Schinken	ham (smoked raw)
gekochter Schinken	cooked ham
Schlachtplatte	mixed cold meat
Speck	bacon
Zunge	tongue

WILD UND GEFLÜGEL	GAME AND POULTRY
Ente	duck
Fasan	pheasant
Gans	goose
Hähnchen/Huhn	chicken
am Spiess	roast
Flügel	wing
Brust	breast
Hase	hare
Hasenpfeffer	jugged hare
(gespickter) Hirsch	(larded) deer
Huhn	chicken
Kaninchen	rabbit
Rebhuhn	partridge
Reh(braten)	(roast) venison
Rehrücken	saddle of deer
Taube	pigeon
Truthahn, Pute	turkey

GEMÜSE UND SALAT	VEGETABLES AND SALAD
Blumenkohl	cauliflower
Bohnen	beans
grüne Bohnen	green beans
Stangenbohnen	runner beans
weisse Bohnen	haricot beans
Brunnenkresse	watercress
Champignons	mushrooms
Edelpilze	(best varieties of wild) mushrooms
Erbsen	peas
Grüner Salat	lettuce
Grünkohl	kale
Gurke	cucumber
Gewürzgurken	pickled cucumbers
Himmel und Erde	potato and apple
Kartoffeln	potatoes
Salzkartoffeln	boiled potatoes
Kartoffelpüree	mashed potatoes
Kartoffelklösse	potato dumplings
Pommes frites	chips
Bratkartoffeln	fried potatoes
Rösti	hashed brown potatoes
Kartoffelsalat	potato salad
Kastanien	chestnuts
Knoblauch	garlic

Kohl (Weiss-, Rot-)	cabbage (white, red)
Kopfsalat	(cabbage) lettuce
Kürbis	pumpkin, marrow
Lauch, Porree	leeks
Meerrettich	horse radish
Paprika (-schoten)	peppers
Pfifferlinge	mushrooms (chanterelle)
Pilze	mushrooms
Reis	rice
Rettich	radish
Rosenkohl	brussels sprouts
Rote Beete	beetroots
Rüben	swedes
Salat	lettuce/salad
Sauerkraut	pickled cabbage
Schwarzwurzeln	scorzonera
Sellerie	celery
Spargel	asparagus
Spinat	spinach
Steinpilze	mushrooms (Boletus edulis, cèpe)
Tomaten	tomatoes
Weisse Rübe	turnip
Wirsingkohl	savoy cabbage

| Wurzeln (Möhren, Karotten) | carrots |
| Zwiebeln | onions |

KNÖDEL	DUMMLINGS AND NOODLES
Leberknödeln	liver dumplings
Kartoffelknödeln	potato dumplings
Klösse	dumplings
Kräuterklösse	herb dumplings
Maultasche	Swabian ravioli
Nockerl	dumpling
Nudeln	noodles
Spätzle	German variety of pasta

EIER	EGGS
gekochtes Ei (weich, hart)	boiled egg (soft, hard)
Omelett	omelette
mit Pilzen	with mushrooms
mit Kräutern	with herbs
Bauernomelett	with diced bacon and onion
Rührei	scrambled eggs
Russische Eier	hard boiled eggs with caviare, capers and mayonnaise
Spiegeleier	fried eggs
verlorene Eier	poached eggs

KÄSE	CHEESE
Allgäuer, Emmentaler	Swiss cheese
Käseteller	cheese board
Kümmelkäse	cheese with caraway seed
Rahmkäse, Sahnekäse	cream cheese
Räucherkäse	smoked cheese
Schmelzkäse	cheese spread
Thüringer Käse, Harzkäse	sausage-shaped cheeses made from curd

NACHSPEISEN UND KUCHEN	DESSERTS AND CAKES
Apfelkuchen	apple cake
Apfelstrudel	flaky pastry stuffed with apple, walnut, spices
Auflauf	soufflé
Eis (Speiseeis):	ice cream:
Erdbeer-	strawberry
gemischtes-	mixed
Mokka-	coffee
Nuss-	nut
Schokoladen-	chocolate
Vanille-	vanilla
Eisbecher	ice cream with fresh fruit
Frisches Obst	fresh fruit
Frucht Törtchen	small fruit tart

Kaiserschmarren	shredded pancake with raisins and syrup
Käsetorte	cheesecake
Keks	biscuit
Krapfen	doughnuts
Kuchen	cake
Lebkuchen	spiced cake, gingerbread
Linzer Torte	cake spread with jam, topped with whipped cream
Makronen	macaroons
Mohrenkopf	pastry filled with cream, topped with chocolate
Mokka Torte	coffee cake
Nusstorte	nut cake
Obstkompott	stewed fruit
Obstkuchen	fruit tart
Obstsalat	fruit salad
Palatschinke	pancake filled either with sausage or with cheese and nuts or with jam
Pfannkuchen	pancakes, doughnuts, fritters
Pfirsich Melba	peach melba
Pflaumenkuchen	plum cake
rote Grütze	raspberries or redcurrants cooked with semolina, served with cream

Sacher Torte	chocolate cake spread with jam and chocolate icing
Sandtorte	Madeira cake
Schlagsahne	whipped cream
Stollen	rich cake with fruit and nuts
Streuselkuchen	cake sprinkled with almonds and cinnamon butter
Torte	tart, flat cake

OBST UND NÜSSE — FRUIT AND NUTS

Ananas	pineapple
Apfel	apple
Apfelsine	orange
Aprikose	apricot
Banane	banana
Birne	pear
Brombeere	blackberry
Erdbeere	strawberry
Feige	fig
Haselnuss	hazelnut
Himbeere	raspberry
Johannisbeere (rot)	red currant
Johannisbeere (schwarz)	blackcurrant
Kirsch	cherry

Mandarine	mandarin orange, tangerine
Mandel	almond
Melone	melon
Pampelmuse	grapefruit
Pfirsich	peach
Pflaume	plum
Reineclaude	greengage
Stachelbeere	gooseberry
(Wein)traube	grape
Walnuss	walnut
Wassermelone	water melon
Zitrone	lemon
Zwetschen	plums

GETRÄNKE

DRINKS

Alkohol	alcohol
Apfelsaft	applejuice
Apfelsinensaft	orange juice
Apfelwein	cider
Bier (hell/dunkel)	beer (light/dark)
Bockbier	bock beer (dark and very strong)
Bowle	fruit cup
Cognac	brandy
(Himbeer)geist	(raspberry) brandy

Glühwein	mulled wine
Grog	grog
Kaffee	coffee
Milchkaffee	white
Schwarzer	black
mit Sahne	with cream
Kaffee Haag (ohne Caffein)	(caffeine free)
Likör	liqueur
Limonade	lemonade
Märzen	strong beer
Milch	milk
Mineralwasser	mineral water
Obstsaft	fruit juice
Orangeade	orangeade
Pilsener	lager
Portwein	port
Rum	rum
Sekt	a German sparkling wine
Schnaps	a German grain spirit
Sherry	sherry
Sodawasser	soda water
Tee	tea
Wasser	water
(Kirsch-/Zwetschen) wasser	(cherry/plum) brandy

Wein	wine
offen	open, by the glass
rot	red
weiss	white
süss	sweet
trocken	dry
Weinbrand	brandy
Wermut	vermouth
Whisky	whisky

SOME COOKING METHODS AND SAUCES

fleisch – rot	meat – rare
halbdurch	medium
durchgebraten	well-done
blau	au bleu
gebacken	baked
gebraten	roast
(in der Pfanne) gebraten	fried
gedämpft	steamed, stewed
gefüllt	stuffed
gegrillt	grilled
gekocht	boiled
geräuchert	smoked
gerieben	grated
geschmort	braised, stewed
geschwenkt	sautéed

mariniert	marinated
... püree	creamed ...
roh	raw
Butter-	buttered ...
Grüne Sauce	mayonnaise (or vinaigrette with chopped egg) with mixed green herbs
Holländisch	with mayonnaise
Holstein	topped with fried egg, garnished with anchovy (the grand version with assorted seafood)
nach Jägerart	sautéed with mushrooms, in wine sauce
Kräuter(butter)	herb (butter)
Petersilien-	parsleyed ...
Sahne-/Rahm-	... and cream
Senf-	mustard ...
Sülz-	... in aspic

Shopping[1] and services

Where to go

Which is the best . . . ?	Welches ist der/die/das beste . . . ?
Where is the nearest . . . ?	Wo ist der/die/das nächste . . . ?
Can you recommend a . . . ?	Können Sie einen/eine/ein . . . empfehlen?
Where is the market?	Wo ist der Markt?
Is there a market every day?	Ist jeden Tag Markt?
Where can I buy . . .	Wo kann ich . . . kaufen?
When are the shops open?	Wann sind die Geschäfte geöffnet?

1. Shopping hours in Germany vary in different parts of the country; generally however shops open at 9 a.m. and close at 6.30 p.m. They are closed on Sundays and public holidays (p. 165) and on Saturday afternoons. In Austria most shops are open from 8 a.m. to 12 noon and from 2 to 6 p.m. and are closed either Wednesday or Saturda afternoon. In Switzerland shops are open from 8 a.m. to 12 noon and from 2 to 6 p.m., closed Saturday afternoons.

antique shop	der Antiquitätenladen	unteekveetayten-lahden
baker	der Backer/die Bäckerei	bucker/beckerī
barber (see p. 123)	der Friseur	freezer
bookshop	die Buchhandlung	bookh-huntloong
butcher (see pp. 97 and 98)	die Metzgerei/die Schlachterei	metsgeri/shlukhterī
chemist (see p. 117)	die Apotheke (*for medicines*)/die Drogerie (*for cosmetics, etc.*)	upohtay-ker/droh-gair-ee
confectioner (see p. 103)	die Konditorei	condeetorī
department store (see pp. 114 and 119)	das Warenhaus	vahrenhows
dry cleaner (see p. 125)	die (chemische) Reinigung	(kaymisher) rynigoong
fishmonger (see p. 96)	die Fischhandlung	fish-huntloong
florist	das Blumengeschäft	bloomen-gesheft
greengrocer (see pp. 100 and 105)	die Gemüsehandlung	gemuise-huntloong
grocer (see p. 122)	das Lebensmittel-geschäft	laybensmittel-gesheft
hairdresser (see p. 123)	der (Damen)friseur	(dahmen)freezer

hardware store (see p. 124)	die Eisenwaren-handlung	Isenvahren-huntlöong
jeweller (see p. 131)	der Juwelier	yööveleer
launderette	die Schnellwä-scherei	shnel-vesherl
laundry (see p. 125)	die Wäscherei	vesherl
liquor/wine store (see p. 106)	die Spirituosen-/Weinhandlung	spee-ree-töö-oh-zen-/vine-huntlöong
newsagent (see p. 126)	die Zeitungshandlung	tsytööngs-huntlöong
optician (see p. 130)	der Optiker	opteekair
shoemaker	der Schuhster	shöö-stair
shoe shop (see p. 119)	das Schuhgeschäft	shöö-gesheft
sports shop	das Sportgeschäft	shport-gesheft
stationer (see p. 127)	das Schreibwaren-geschäft	shripvahren-gesheft
supermarket	der Supermarkt	zuper-murkt
tobacconist (see p. 129)	der Tabakladen	tubuck-lahden
toy shop	das Spielwaren-geschäft	shpeelvahren-gesheft

In the shop

Self service	*Selbstbedienung
Sale (clearance)	*Schlussverkauf/Ausverkauf
Cash desk	*Kasse
Shop assistant	Der Verkäufer/die Verkäuferin
Manager	Der Geschäftsführer
Can I help you?	*Was darf es sein?
I want to buy . . .	Ich möchte . . . kaufen
Do you sell . . .?	Verkaufen Sie . . .?
I'm just looking round	Ich möchte mich nur umsehen
I don't want to buy anything now	Ich möchte im Augenblick nichts kaufen
Could you show me . . .?	Könnten Sie mir bitte . . . zeigen?
We do not have that	*Das haben wir leider nicht
You'll find them at that counter	*Sie sind dort auf dem Verkaufstisch
We've sold out but we'll have more tomorrow	*Wir sind im Augenblick ausverkauft, aber morgen haben wir mehr
Anything else?	*Sonst noch etwas?
That will be all	Das ist alles
Will you take it with you?	*Möchten Sie es mitnehmen?
I will take it with me	Ich nehme es gleich mit

Please send it to this address/X hotel	Bitte schicken Sie es an diese Adresse/ins Hotel X

Choosing

I want something in leather/green	Ich möchte etwas aus Leder/in grün
I need it to match this	Es soll hierzu passen
I like the one in the window	Das im Fenster gefällt mir
Could I see that one, please?	Darf ich das mal sehen, bitte?
I like the colour but not the style	Mir gefällt die Farbe, aber nicht der Schnitt
I want a darker/lighter shade	Ich möchte einen dunkleren/helleren Farbton
I need something warmer/thinner	Ich brauche etwas Wärmeres/Dünneres
Do you have one in another colour/size?	Haben Sie es in einer anderen Farbe/Grösse?
Have you anything better/cheaper?	Haben Sie etwas Besseres/Billigeres?
How much is this?	Was kostet das?
That is too much for me	Das ist mir zu teuer
What's it made of?	Woraus ist es gemacht?
What size is this?	Welche Grösse ist das?

I take size[1] ...	Ich brauche Grösse ...
The English/American size is ...	Die englische/amerikanische Grösse ist ...
My collar/chest/waist is ...	Meine Kragenweite/mein Brustumfang/meine Taillenweite ist ...
Can I try it on?	Kann ich es anprobieren?
It's too short/long/tight/loose	Es ist zu kurz/lang/eng/weit
Have you a larger one/smaller one?	Haben Sie ein grösseres/ kleineres

Colours

beige	beige	behj
black	schwarz	shvurts
blue	blau	blow
brown	braun	brown
gold	golden	gohlden
green	grün	gruin
grey	grau	grow
mauve	lila	leelah
orange	orangenfarbig	orunjenfurbikh
pink	rosa	rozah

1. See table (p. 120) for continental sizes.

purple	purpur	pōōrpōōr
red	rot	roht
silver	silbern	zilbairn
white	weiss	vis
yellow	gelb	gelp

Complaints

I want to see the manager	Ich möchte den Geschäftsführer sprechen
I bought this yesterday	Ich habe dies gestern gekauft
It doesn't work/fit	Es funktioniert/passt nicht
This is dirty/torn/broken/bad	Es ist schmutzig/zerrissen/kaputt/schlecht
This is stained/cracked	Es hat Flecken/einen Sprung
Will you change it please?	Können Sie es bitte umtauschen?
Will you refund my money?	Können Sie mir bitte mein Geld zurückgeben?
Here is the receipt	Hier ist die Quittung

Paying

How much is this?	Wie teuer ist das?
That's 10 DM, please	*Das macht zehn Mark bitte
They are one mark each	*Sie kosten eine Mark pro Stück
How much does that come to?	Was macht das?
That will be ...	*Das macht ...
Can I pay with English/American currency?	Nehmen Sie englisches/ amerikanisches Geld?
Do you take credit cards/ traveller's cheques?	Nehmen Sie Kreditkarten/ Reiseschecks?
Please pay the cashier	*Bitte, zahlen Sie an der Kasse
May I have a receipt, please	Kann ich bitte eine Quittung haben?
You've given me too little/too much change	Sie haben mir zu wenig/zu viel Geld herausgegeben

Chemist[1]

Can you prepare this prescription for me, please?	Können Sie bitte dieses Rezept für mich zubereiten?
Have you a small first-aid kit?	Haben Sie einen kleinen Verbandkasten?
I want some aspirin/sun cream (for children)	Ich möchte Aspirin/ Sonnencreme (für Kinder)

1. You go to an Apotheke for prescriptions, medicines, etc., and to a Drogerie for toilet requisites.

A tin of adhesive plaster	Eine Schachtel Hansaplast/ Heftpflaster
Can you suggest something for indigestion/constipation/ diarrhoea?	Können Sie etwas vorschlagen gegen Verdauungsstörung/ Verstopfung/Durchfall
I want something for insect bites	Ich möchte etwas gegen Insektenstiche
Can you give me something for sunburn?	Können Sie mir etwas gegen Sonnenbrand geben?
I want some throat lozenges/ stomach pills/antiseptic cream/ lipsalve	Ich brauche Halspastillen/ Magentabletten/ antiseptische Creme/ Lippensalbe
Do you have sanitary towels/ tampons/cotton wool?	Haben Sie Binden/Tampons/ Watte?
I need something for insect bites/ a hangover/travel sickness	Ich brauche etwas für Insektenstiche/einen Kater/ Reiseübelkeit

Toilet requisites[1]

A packet of razor blades, please	Eine Schachtel Rasierklingen bitte
How much is this after-shave lotion?	Wie teuer ist dieses Rasierwasser?
A tube of toothpaste, please	Eine Tube Zahnpasta bitte

1. You go to an Apotheke for prescriptions, medicines, etc., and to a Drogerie for toilet requisites.

A box of paper handkerchiefs/a roll of toilet paper, please	Eine Schachtel Papiertaschentücher/eine Rolle Toilettenpapier, bitte
I want some eau-de-cologne/perfume/cream	Ich möchte Kölnisch Wasser/Parfüm/Creme
May I try it?	Kann ich es ausprobieren?
What kinds of soap have you?	Welche Arten von Seife haben Sie?
A bottle/tube of shampoo, please, for dry/greasy hair	Eine Flasche/Tube Schampoo bitte für trockenes/fettiges Haar
Do you have any suntan oil/cream?	Haben Sie Sonnenöl/Sonnencreme?

Clothes and shoes[1]

I want a hat/sunhat	Ich möchte einen Hut/Sonnenhut
Can I see some dresses, please?	Kann ich mir bitte einige Kleider ansehen?
Where is the underwear/haberdashery/coats department?	Wo ist die Unterwäsche-/Kurzwaren-/Mantel-abteilung?
Where are beach clothes?	Wo finde ich Strandkleidung?

1. For sizes see p. 120.

I want a short/long sleeved shirt, collar size ...	Ich möchte ein Hemd mit kurzen/langen Ärmeln, Kragenweite ...
Where can I find socks/stockings?	Wo finde ich Socken/Strümpfe?
I am looking for a blouse/bra/dress/jumper	Ich suche eine Bluse/einen Beha/ein Kleid/einen Pullover
I need a coat/raincoat/jacket	Ich brauche einen Mantel/Regenmantel/eine Jacke
Do you sell buttons/elastic/zips?	Verkaufen Sie Knöpfe/Gummiband/Reissverschlüsse?
I need a pair of walking shoes/beach sandals/black shoes	Ich brauche ein Paar Strassenschuhe/Strandsandalen/schwarze Schuhe
These heels are too high/too low	Diese Absätze sind zu hoch/zu niedrig

Clothing sizes

WOMEN'S DRESSES, ETC.

British	32	34	36	38	40	42	44
American	10	12	14	16	18	20	22
Continental	30	32	34	36	38	40	42

MEN'S PULLOVERS, ETC.

British and American	36	38	40	42	44	46
Continental	46	48	50	52	54	56

MEN'S SHIRTS:

British and American	13	13½	14	14½	15	15½	15¾	16	16½	17	17½
Continental	34	35	36	37	38	39	40	41	42	43	44

MEN'S SOCKS:

British and American	10	10½	11	11½	12
Continental	39–40	41–42	43–44	45–46	47–48

STOCKINGS:

British and American	8	8½	9	9½	10	10½	11
Continental	0	1	2	3	4	5	6

SHOES:

British	1	2	3	4	5	6	7	8	9	10	11	12
American	2½	3½	4½	5½	6½	7½	8½	9½	10½	11½	12½	13½
Continental	33	34/5	36	37	38	39/40	41	42	43	44	45	46

Food[1]

Give me a kilo/half a kilo (pound) of . . . please	Geben Sie mir bitte ein Kilo/ ein halbes Kilo (ein Pfund) . . .
I want some sweets/chocolates, please	Ich möchte bitte Bonbons/ Pralinen
A bottle of milk/wine/beer, please	Eine Flasche Milch/Wein/Bier bitte
Is there anything back on the bottle?	Bekomme ich für die Flasche Pfand zurück?
I want a jar/tin (can)/packet of . . .	Ich möchte ein Glas/eine Dose/ ein Paket . . .
Do you sell frozen foods?	Verkaufen Sie Tiefkühlkost?
These pears are too hard/soft	Diese Birnen sind zu hart/weich
Is it fresh?	Ist es frisch?
Are they ripe?	Sind sie reif?
This is bad/stale	Dies ist schlecht/alt
A loaf of bread, please	Ein Brot bitte
Dark ryebread	Vollkornbrot/Schwarzbrot
Ryebread	Graubrot
White bread	Weissbrot
How much a kilo/bottle?	Wie teuer ist ein Kilo/eine Flasche?

1. See also the various MENU sections (p. 94 onward) and WEIGHTS AND
MEASURES, pp. 173–4.

Hairdresser and barber

May I make an appointment for this morning/tomorrow afternoon?	Kann ich mich für heute morgen/morgen nachmittag anmelden?
What time?	Zu welcher Zeit?
I want my hair cut	Ich möchte mir die Haare schneiden lassen
I want my hair trimmed	Schneiden Sie mein Haar bitte nur ein wenig kürzer
Not too short at the sides	Nicht zu kurz an den Seiten
I'll have it shorter at the back, please	Hinten möchte ich es bitte kürzer haben
My hair is oily/dry	Mein Haar ist fettig/trocken
I want a shampoo	Waschen bitte
I want my hair washed and set	Waschen und legen bitte
Please set it without rollers/on large/small rollers	Bitte legen Sie es ohne Lockenwickler/auf grosse/kleine Lockenwickler
Please do not use any hairspray	Bitte benutzen Sie keinen Haarspray
I want a colour rinse	Ich möchte einen Farbfestiger
I'd like to see a colour chart	Kann ich bitte eine Farbskala sehen
I want a darker/lighter shade	Ich möchte einen dunkleren/helleren Farbton

I'd like it set this way, please	Ich möchte es bitte so gelegt haben
The water is too cold	Das Wasser ist zu kalt
The dryer is too hot	Die Trockenhaube ist zu heiss
Thank you, I like it very much	Danke, so gefällt es mir gut
I want a shave/manicure	Ich möchte mich rasieren/maniküren lassen

Hardware

Where is the camping equipment?	Wo ist die Camping/Zelt Ausrüstung?
Do you have a battery for this?	Haben Sie hierfür eine Batterie?
Where can I get butane gas/paraffin?	Wo kann ich Butan Gas/Petroleum bekommen?
I need a bottle opener/tin opener/corkscrew	Ich brauche einen Flaschenöffner/Dosenöffner/Korkenzieher
A small/large screwdriver	Ein kleiner/grosser Schraubenzieher
I'd like some candles/matches	Ich möchte Kerzen/Streichhölzer
I want a flashlight/(pen) knife/pair of scissors	Ich möchte eine Taschenlampe/ein (Taschen)messer/eine Schere

Do you sell string/rope?	Verkaufen Sie Band/Tau?
Where can I find washing-up liquid/scouring powder/soap pads?	Wo finde ich Abwaschseife/Scheuersand/Seifenkissen?
Do you have a dishcloth/brush?	Haben Sie ein Geschirrtuch/eine Bürste?
I need a groundsheet/bucket/frying pan	Ich brauche eine Zeltbahn/einen Eimer/eine Bratpfanne

Laundry and dry cleaning

Where is the nearest launderette/dry cleaner?	Wo ist die nächste Schnellwäscherei/Reinigung?
I want to have these things washed/cleaned	Ich möchte diese Sachen waschen lassen/reinigen lassen
These stains won't come out	*Diese Flecken gehen nicht raus
Can you get this stain out?	Können Sie diesen Flecken rausmachen?
It is coffee/wine/grease	Es ist Kaffee/Wein/Fett
When will they be ready?	Wann sind sie fertig?
It only needs to be pressed	Es muss nur geplättet (gebügelt) werden
This is torn, can you mend it?	Dies ist zerrissen, können Sie es ausbessern?
Do you do invisible mending?	Machen Sie Kunststopfen?

There's a button missing	Hier fehlt ein Knopf
Will you sew on another one, please?	Würden Sie bitte einen anderen annähen?
I need them by this evening/tomorrow	Ich brauche sie bis heute Abend/Morgen
Call back at five o'clock	*Kommen Sie um fünf Uhr wieder
We can't do it until Tuesday	*Wir können es nicht vor Dienstag machen
It will take three days	*Es dauert drei Tage

Newspapers, writing materials and records

Do you sell English/American newspapers/magazines?	Verkaufen Sie englische/amerikanische Zeitungen/Zeitschriften?
Can you get . . . magazine for me?	Können Sie die Zeitschrift . . . für mich besorgen?
Where can I get the . . .?	Wo kann ich . . . bekommen?
I want a map of the city/road map of . . .	Ich möchte einen Stadtplan/Strassenplan von . . .
I want an entertainment/amusements guide	Ich möchte ein Veranstaltungsprogramm
Do you have any English books?	Haben Sie englische Bücher?

Have you any books by . . .?	Haben Sie irgendwelche Bücher von . . .?
I want some picture postcards/ plain postcards	Ich möchte einige Ansichtskarten/Postkarten
Do you sell souvenirs/toys?	Verkaufen Sie Reiseandenken/ Spielwaren?
Do you have any records of local music?	Haben Sie Platten mit hiesiger Musik?
Can I listen to this record, please?	Kann ich mir bitte diese Platte anhören?
Are there any new records by . . .	Gibt es neue Platten von . . .?
ballpoint	der Kugelschreiber
cellotape	Tesafilm
drawing pin	die Reisszwecke
elastic band	das Gummiband
envelope	der Umschlag, das Kuvert
glue/paste	der Leim/Klebstoff
ink	die Tinte
(coloured) pencil	der Bleistift (Farbstift)
string	das Band
(writing) paper	das (Schreib)papier

Photography

I want to buy a camera	Ich möchte eine Kamera kaufen
Have you a film/cartridge for this camera, please?	Haben Sie einen Film/eine Filmpatrone für diesen (Foto)apparat?
A 120/126 spool film, please, with 20/36 exposures	Einen hundert zwanzig/hundert sechsundzwanzig Film, bitte, mit zwanzig/sechsunddreissig Aufnahmen
Give me an 8/16/35 mm film, please	Geben Sie mir bitte einen acht/sechzehn/fünfunddreissig Millimeter Film
I want a (fast) colour film/black-and-white film	Ich möchte einen (schnellen) Farbfilm/schwarz-weiss Film
Would you fit the film in the camera for me, please	Würden Sie bitte den Film für mich in den Apparat einlegen
Do you have flash bulbs/cubes?	Haben Sie Blitzlampen/Blitzwürfel?
Does the price include processing?	Schliesst dieser Preis das Entwickeln ein?
I'd like this film developed and printed	Würden Sie diesen Film bitte entwickeln und abziehen?
Please enlarge this negative	Bitte machen Sie eine Vergrösserung von diesem Negativ
When will it be ready?	Wann ist es fertig?

Will it be done tomorrow?	Ist es morgen fertig?
My camera's not working, can you mend it?	Meine Kamera funktioniert nicht, können Sie sie reparieren?
The film is jammed	Der Film hat sich festgeklemmt
There is something wrong with the shutter/light meter/film winder	Es stimmt etwas nicht mit dem Verschluss/Belichtungsmesser/Transportknopf
I need a (haze) filter/lens cap	Ich brauche einen (Dunst) Filter/Objektivdeckel

Tobacconist

Do you stock English/American cigarettes?	Haben Sie englische/amerikanische Zigaretten?
What cigarettes/cigars have you?	Welche Zigaretten/Zigarren haben Sie?
A packet of . . . please	Eine Schachtel . . . bitte
I want some filter tip cigarettes/cigarettes without filter/menthol cigarettes	Ich möchte Filterzigaretten/Zigaretten ohne Filter/Zigaretten mit Menthol
A box of matches, please	Eine Schachtel Streichhölzer bitte
Do you have cigarette paper/pipe cleaners?	Haben Sie Zigarettenpapier/Pfeifenreiniger?

I want to buy a lighter — Ich möchte ein Feuerzeug kaufen

Do you sell lighter fuel/flints? — Verkaufen Sie Feuerzeug-Benzin/Flintsteine?

I want a gas refill — Ich möchte eine neue Gasfüllung

Repairs

This is broken; could you mend it? — Dies ist kaputt; können Sie es reparieren?

Could you do it while I wait? — Können Sie es machen, während ich warte?

When should I come back for it? — Wann kann ich es abholen?

I want these shoes soled (with leather) — Ich möchte an diesen Schuhen (Leder)sohlen haben

I want them heeled (with rubber) — Ich möchte an ihnen (Gummi)absätze haben

I have broken the heel; can you put on a new one? — Der Absatz ist gebrochen; können Sie einen neuen anmachen?

My watch is broken — Meine Uhr ist kaputt

I have broken the glass/strap/spring — Das Glas/der Riemen/die Feder ist kaputt

I have broken my glasses/the frame/the arm — Meine Brille/der Rahmen/der Bügel ist kaputt

How much would a new one cost?	Wieviel kostet ein neuer/eine neue/ein neues?
The stone/charm/screw has come loose	Der Stein/der Anhänger/die Schraube ist lose
The fastener/clip/chain is broken	Der Verschluss/die Spange/die Kette ist kaputt
It can't be repaired	*Es kann nicht repariert werden

Post Office

Where's the main post office?	Wo ist die Hauptpost?
Where's the nearest post office?	Wo ist die nächste Post?
What time does the post office open/close?	Wann macht die Post auf/zu?
Where's the post box?	Wo ist der Briefkasten?
Which window do I go to for stamps/money orders?	An welchem Fenster bekomme ich Briefmarken/ Postanweisungen?
Where can I send a telegram?	Wo kann ich ein Telegram aufgeben?

Letters and telegrams

How much is a postcard to England?	Wie teuer ist eine Postkarte nach England?
What's the airmail to the USA?	Wie teuer ist Luftpost in die USA?
How much is it to send a letter surface mail to the USA?	Wie teuer ist ein Brief per Schiffpost in die USA?
It's inland	Es ist fürs Inland
Give me three . . . pfennig stamps, please	Geben Sie mir bitte drei Briefmarken zu . . . Pfennig
I want to send this letter express	Ich möchte diesen Brief per Eilpost senden
I want to register this letter	Ich möchte diesen Brief einschreiben
Two airmail forms, please	Zwei Luftpostbriefe bitte
Where is the poste restante section?	Wo ist der Schalter 'Postlagernde Sendungen'?
Are there any letters for me?	Sind Briefe für mich da?
What is your name?	*Wie ist Ihr Name?
Have you any means of identification?	*Können Sie sich identifizieren (ausweisen)?
I want to send a (reply paid) telegram/night letter	Ich möchte ein Telegramm (mit bezahlter Antwort)/ein Brieftelegramm senden

How much does it cost per word?	Wieviel kostet es pro Wort?
Write the message here and your own name and address	*Schreiben Sie den Text hier und Ihren eigenen Namen und Adresse

Telephoning

Where's the nearest phone box?	Wo ist die nächste Telefonzelle?
I want to make a phone call	Ich möchte telefonieren
May I use your phone?	Kann ich Ihr Telefon benutzen?
Do you have a telephone directory for . . .?	Haben Sie ein Telefonbuch für . . .?
Please get me . . .	Bitte verbinden Sie mich mit . . .
I want to telephone to England	Ich möchte nach England telefonieren
I want to make a personal (person-to-person) call	Ich möchte ein V-Gespräch führen (*pronounce* V *as vow*)
Could you give me the cost (time and charges) afterwards?	Könnten Sie mir hinterher die Gebühren angeben?
I want to reverse the charges (call collect)	Ein R-Gespräch bitte (*pronounce* R *as air*)
I was cut off; can you reconnect me?	Ich wurde unterbrochen; können Sie mich wieder verbinden?
I want extension . . .	Apparat . . . bitte

May I speak to . . .	Kann ich bitte . . . sprechen
Who's speaking?	*Wer spricht da?
Hold the line, please	*Bleiben Sie bitte am Apparat
Put the receiver down	*Legen Sie den Hörer auf
He's not here	*Er ist nicht hier
When will he be back?	Wann kommt er zurück?
Will you take a message?	Würden Sie bitte etwas ausrichten?
Tell him that . . . phoned	Sagen Sie ihm bitte, dass . . . angerufen hat
I'll ring again later	Ich rufe später wieder an
Please ask him to phone me	Bitten Sie ihn, mich anzurufen
What's your number?	*Wie ist Ihre Nummer?
My number is . . .	Meine Nummer ist . . .
I can't hear you	Ich kann Sie nicht verstehen
The line is engaged	*Die Leitung ist besetzt
There's no reply	*Es meldet sich niemand
You have the wrong number	*Sie sind falsch verbunden

Sightseeing[1]

What ought one to see here?	Was ist hier sehenswert?
Is there a sightseeing tour/boat ride?	Gibt es eine Stadtrundfahrt/ Bootsfahrt?
What's this building?	Was ist das für ein Gebäude?
Which is the oldest building in the city?	Welches ist das älteste Gebäude in der Stadt?
When was it built?	Wann wurde es gebaut?
Who built it?	Wer hat es gebaut?
What's the name of this church?	Wie heisst diese Kirche?
Is this the natural history museum?	Ist dies das Naturkunde- Museum?
When is the museum open?	Wann ist das Museum geöffnet?
Is it open on Sundays?	Ist es sonntags geöffnet?
The museum is closed on Mondays	*Das Museum ist montags geschlossen

1. See also BUS and COACH TRAVEL (p. 54), DIRECTIONS (p. 57).

Admission free	*Eintritt frei
How much is it to go in?	Wieviel Eintritt kostet es?
Are there reductions for children/students?	Gibt es Ermässigung für Kinder/Studenten?
Are the entry fees reduced on any special day?	Gibt es an bestimmten Tagen eine Eintrittsermässigung?
Have you a ticket?	*Haben Sie eine Eintrittskarte?
Where do I get tickets?	Wo bekomme ich Eintrittskarten?
Please leave your bag in the cloakroom	*Bitte lassen Sie Ihre Tasche in der Garderobe
It's over there	*Es ist dort drüben
Can I take pictures?	Kann ich fotografieren?
Photographs are prohibited	*Fotografieren ist verboten
Follow the guide	*Folgen Sie dem Führer
Does the guide speak English?	Spricht der Führer englisch?
We don't need a guide	Wir brauchen keinen Fuhrer
Where is the . . . collection/exhibition?	Wo ist die Sammlung/Ausstellung . . .?
Where are the Rembrandts?	Wo sind die Rembrandts?
Where can I get a catalogue?	Wo kann ich einen Katalog bekommen?
Where can I get a plan/guide book of the city?	Wo kann ich einen Stadtplan/Stadtführer bekommen?
Is this the way to the zoo?	Komme ich hier zum Zoo?
Which bus goes to the castle?	Welcher Bus fährt zum Schloss?

How do I get to the park?	Wie komme ich zum Park?
Where do we find antiques/ souvenirs/a shopping centre/the market?	Wo gibt es Antiquitäten/ Reiseandenken/ein Einkaufszentrum/den Markt?
Can we walk it?	Können wir zu Fuss gehen?

Entertainment

Is there an entertainment guide?	Gibt es ein Veranstaltungsprogramm?
What's on at the theatre/cinema?	Was wird im Theater/im Kino gespielt?
Is there a concert on?	Gibt es ein Konzert?
I want two seats for tonight/ for the matinee tomorrow	Ich möchte zwei Plätze für heute Abend/für die Matinee-Vorstellung morgen
I want to book seats for Thursday	Ich möchte Plätze für Donnerstag bestellen
That performance is sold out	*Die Vorstellung ist ausverkauft
Are they good seats?	Sind es gute Plätze?
Where are these seats?	Wo sind diese Plätze?
When does the curtain go up?	Wann geht der Vorhang auf?
What time does the performance end?	Wann ist die Vorstellung zu Ende?
Is evening dress necessary?	Ist Abendkleidung erforderlich?

Where is the cloakroom?   Wo ist die Garderobe?

This is your seat   *Hier ist Ihr Platz

A programme, please   Ein Programm bitte

What's the best nightclub?   Welches ist der beste Nachtklub?

What time is the floorshow?   Wann beginnt das Kabarett?

May I have this dance?   Darf ich Sie um diesen Tanz bitten?

Is there a jazz club here?   Gibt es hier einen Jazz Club?

Do you have a discotheque here?   Haben Sie hier eine Diskothek?

Can you recommend a good show?   Können Sie eine gute Veranstaltung empfehlen?

Sports and games

Where is the nearest tennis court/ golf course?	Wo ist der nächste Tennisplatz/ Golfplatz?
What is the charge per game/ hour/day?	Wieviel kostet es pro Spiel/ Stunde/Tag?
Where can we go swimming/ fishing?	Wo können wir schwimmen/ angeln?
Can I hire a racket/clubs/fishing tackle?	Kann ich einen Tennisschläger/ Golfschläger/ein Angelgerät mieten?
I want to go fishing; do I need a permit?	Ich möchte angeln gehen; brauche ich einen Angelschein?
Where do I get a permit?	Wo bekomme ich einen (Angel)schein?
Is there a skating rink/ski slope?	Gibt es eine Eisbahn/einen Skiabhang?
Can I hire skates/skiing equipment?	Kann ich Schlittschuhe/eine Skiausrüstung leihen?

Are there ski lifts?	Gibt es Skilifts?
Can I take lessons here?	Kann ich hier Unterricht nehmen?
Where is the stadium?	Wo ist das Stadion?
Are there any seats left in the grandstand?	Gibt es noch Plätze auf der Haupttribüne?
How much are the cheapest seats?	Wieviel kosten die billigsten Plätze?
Are the seats in the sun/shade?	Sind die Plätze in der Sonne/im Schatten?
We want to go to a football match/a tennis tournament	Wir möchten uns ein Fussballspiel/ein Tennisturnier ansehen
Who's playing?	Wer spielt?
When does it start?	Wann fängt es an?
What is the score?	Wie steht's?
Who's winning?	Wer gewinnt?
Where's the race course?	Wo ist die Rennbahn?
When's the next meeting?	Wann ist das nächste Rennen?
Which is the favourite?	Wer ist der Favorit?
Who's the jockey?	Wer ist der Jockey?
20 DM to win on . . ./each way on . . .	Zwanzig Mark Siegwette auf . . ./ Sieg- und Platzwette auf . . .
What are the odds?	Wie ist der Wettkurs?
Do you play cards?	Spielen Sie Karten?
Would you like a game of chess?	Möchten Sie Schach spielen?

On the beach

Which is the best beach?	Welches ist der beste Strand?
Is there a quiet beach near here?	Gibt es einen ruhigen Strand in der Nähe?
Is it far to walk?	Ist es weit zu gehen?
Is there a bus to the beach?	Fährt ein Bus zum Strand?
Is the beach sand/pebbles/rocks?	Ist es ein Sand-/Kies-/Felsstrand?
Is the bathing safe from this beach/bay?	Ist das Baden an diesem Strand/in dieser Bucht ungefährlich?
Is it safe for small children?	Können kleine Kinder hier ohne Gefahr baden?
Bathing prohibited/at own risk	*Baden verboten/auf eigene Gefahr
Does it get very rough?	Wird das Wasser sehr bewegt?
It's dangerous	*Es ist gefährlich
Is the tide rising/falling?	Steigt/fällt das Wasser?

There's a strong current here	*Die Strömung ist hier sehr stark
It's very deep here	*Es ist hier sehr tief
Are you a strong swimmer?	*Sind Sie ein tüchtiger Schwimmer?
Is it deep?	Ist es tief?
How's the water? Cold?	Wie ist das Wasser? Kalt?
It's warm	Es ist warm
Can one swim in the lake/river?	Kann man im See/im Fluss baden?
Is there an indoor/outdoor swimming pool?	Gibt es ein Hallenbad/ein Freibad?
Is it salt or fresh water?	Ist es Salz- oder Süsswasser?
Are there showers?	Gibt es Duschen?
I want to hire a cabin for the day/morning/two hours	Ich mochte eine Kabine mieten für den Tag/für den Morgen/für zwei Stunden
I want to hire a deckchair/a sunshade	Ich möchte einen Liegestuhl/Sonnenschirm mieten
Can we water ski here?	Können wir hier Wasserski laufen?
Can we hire the equipment?	Können wir die Ausrüstung mieten?
Where's the harbour?	Wo ist der Hafen?
Can we go out in a fishing boat?	Können wir in einem Fischkutter hinausfahren?

Is there any underwater fishing?	Kann man unter Wasser fischen?
Can I hire skin-diving equipment/a snorkel/flippers?	Kann ich eine Tauchausrüstung/ einen Schnorchel/ Schwimmflossen mieten?
Can I hire a rowing/motor/ sailing boat?	Kann ich ein Ruderboot/ Motorboot/Segelboot mieten?
What does it cost by the hour?	Wieviel kostet ein Boot pro Stunde?

Camping and walking[1]

How long is the walk to the Youth Hostel?	Wie lange geht man zur Jugendherberge?
How far is the next village?	Wie weit ist es bis zum nächsten Dorf?
Is there a footpath to . . .?	Gibt es einen Wanderweg nach . . .?
Is it possible to go across country?	Kann man feldein gehen?
Is there a short cut?	Gibt es einen kürzeren Weg?
It's an hour's walk to . . .	*Man geht eine Stunde nach . . .
Is there a camping site near here?	Gibt es einen Zeltplatz in der Nähe?
Is this an authorized camp site?	Ist das Zelten hier erlaubt?
Are drinking water/lavatories/ showers provided?	Gibt es Trinkwasser/Toiletten/ Duschen?
May we camp here?	Dürfen wir hier zelten?

1. See also DIRECTIONS (p. 57).

Can we hire a tent?

Can we park our caravan here?

What does it cost per person/day/ week?

What is the charge for a tent/ caravan?

Is this drinking water?

Where are the shops?

Where can I buy paraffin/ butane gas?

May we light a fire?

Where do I get rid of rubbish?

Können wir ein Zelt mieten?

Können wir unseren Wohnwagen hier parken?

Was kostet es pro Person/Tag/ Woche?

Wie hoch ist die Gebühr für ein Zelt/einen Wohnwagen?

Ist dies Trinkwasser?

Wo sind die Geschäfte?

Wo kann ich Petroleum/Butan (Gas) kaufen?

Dürfen wir ein Feuer anzünden?

Wo kann ich den Abfall hintun?

At the doctor's

Ailments

Is there a doctor's surgery near here?

Gibt es hier in der Nähe eine Arztpraxis?

I must see a doctor, can you recommend one?

Ich muss zum Arzt, können Sie mir einen empfehlen?

Please call a doctor

Bitte, rufen Sie einen Arzt

I am ill

Ich bin krank

I have a fever

Ich habe Fieber

I've a pain in my right arm

Ich habe Schmerzen im rechten Arm

My wrist hurts

Mein Handgelenk tut mir weh

I think I've sprained my ankle/ broken my ankle

Ich glaube, ich habe mir den Fuss verstaucht/den Knöchel gebrochen

I fell down and hurt my back

Ich bin hingefallen und habe mir den Rücken verletzt

My foot is swollen	Mein Fuss ist geschwollen
I've burned/cut/bruised myself	Ich habe mich verbrannt/geschnitten/gestossen, gequetscht
My stomach is upset	Ich habe Magenbeschwerden
My appetite's gone	Ich habe den Appetit verloren
I think I've got food poisoning	Ich glaube, ich habe eine Lebensmittelvergiftung
I can't eat/sleep	Ich kann nicht essen/nicht schlafen
My nose keeps bleeding	Meine Nase blutet immer
I have difficulty in breathing	Ich habe Schwierigkeiten beim Atmen
I feel dizzy/sick	Mir ist schwindlig/schlecht
I feel shivery	Mich fröstelt
I keep vomiting	Ich muss mich immer übergeben
I think I've caught 'flu	Ich glaube, ich habe Grippe
I've got a cold	Ich habe eine Erkältung
I've had it since yesterday/for a few hours	Ich habe es seit gestern/ein paar Stunden

abscess	das Geschwür	geshvuir
ache	der Schmerz	shmairts
allergy	die Allergie	ullairgee
appendicitis	die Blinddarm-Entzündung	blintdahrm-enttsuindööng

asthma	das Asthma	ustmah
blister	die Blase	blahzer
boil	der Furunkel	fooroonkel
bruise	die Quetschung	kvetshoong
burn	die Brandwunde	bruntvoonder
cardiac condition	der Herzfehler	hairts-faylair
chill, cold	die Erkältung	airkailtoong
constipation	die Verstopfung	fairshtopfoong
cough	der Husten	hoosten
cramp	der Krampf	crumpf
diabetic	zuckerkrank	tsoockercrunk
diarrhoea	der Durchfall	doorkhful
earache	die Ohrenschmerzen	ohrenshmairtsen
fever	das Fieber	feebair
food poisoning	die Lebensmittel-Vergiftung	laybensmittel-fairgiftoong
fracture	der Bruch	brookh
hay-fever	der Heuschnupfen	hoyshnoopfen
headache	die Kopfschmerzen	copfshmairtsen
ill, sick	krank	crunk
illness	die Krankheit	crunkhite
indigestion	die Verdauungs-Störung	fairdowoongs-shter-roong
infection	die Ansteckung	unshteckoong

influenza	die Grippe	**gripper**
insomnia	die Schlaflosigkeit	**shlahf-lohsikh-kite**
itch	das Jucken	**yōōken**
nausea	die Übelkeit	**uibel-kite**
pain	der Schmerz	**shmairts**
rheumatism	der Rheumatismus	**rōōmatizmōōs**
sore throat	die Halsschmerzen	**huls-shmairtsen**
sprain	die Verstauchung	**fairshtowkhōōng**
stomach ache	die Magenschmerzen	**mahgen-shmairtsen**
sunburn	der Sonnenbrand	**zonnen-brunt**
sunstroke	der Sonnenstich	**zonnen-shtikh**
tonsillitis	die Mandel- entzündung	**mundel- enttsuindōōng**
toothache	die Zahnschmerzen	**tsahn-shmairtsen**
ulcer	das Geschwür	**geshvuir**
wound	die Wunde	**vōōnder**

Treatment

You're hurting me	Sie tun mir weh
Must I stay in bed?	Muss ich im Bett bleiben?
Will you call again?	Kommen Sie wieder?
How much do I owe you?	Wieviel schulde ich Ihnen?

When can I travel again?	Wann kann ich wieder reisen?
I feel better now	Mir geht es jetzt wieder besser
Do you have a temperature?	*Haben Sie erhöhte Temperatur?
Where does it hurt?	*Wo tut es weh?
Have you a pain here?	*Haben Sie hier Schmerzen?
How long have you had the pain?	*Seit wann haben Sie die Schmerzen?
Does that hurt?	*Tut das weh?
A lot?	*Sehr?
A little?	*Ein wenig?
Open your mouth	*Machen Sie den Mund auf
Put out your tongue	*Stecken Sie die Zunge raus
Breathe in/out	*Atmen Sie ein/aus
Please lie down	*Legen Sie sich bitte hin
I will need a specimen	*Ich brauche eine Urinprobe
What medicines have you been taking?	*Welche Medikamente haben Sie eingenommen?
I take this medicine; could you give me another prescription?	Ich nehme dieses Medikament ein; können Sie mir noch ein Rezept geben?
I'll give you some pills/tablets/medicine	*Ich werde Ihnen Pillen/Tabletten/Arznei (Medizin) geben
I will give you an antibiotic/sedative	*Ich gebe Ihnen ein Antibiotikum/ein Beruhigungsmittel

Take this prescription to the chemist's	*Bringen Sie dieses Rezept in die Apotheke
Take this three times a day	*Nehmen Sie dies dreimal täglich ein
I'll give you an injection	*Ich gebe Ihnen eine Spritze
Roll up your sleeve	*Rollen Sie den Ärmel auf
I'll put you on a diet	*Ich werde Sie auf Diät setzen
Come and see me again in two days' time	*Kommen Sie in zwei Tagen wieder
Your leg must be X-rayed	*Ihr Bein muss geröntgt werden
You must go to hospital	*Sie müssen ins Krankenhaus
You must stay in bed	*Sie müssen im Bett bleiben
You should not travel until . . .	*Sie sollten bis . . . nicht reisen
Nothing to worry about	*Es besteht kein Grund zur Unruhe

ambulance	der Krankenwagen	crunken-vahgen
anaesthetic	das Betäubungsmittel	betoybööngs-mittell
aspirin	das Aspirin	uspeereen
bandage	der Verband	fairbunt
chiropodist	der Fusspfleger	föös-pflaygair
hospital	das Krankenhaus	crunkenhows
injection	die Spritze	shprittser
laxative	das Abführmittel	upfuir-mittell
nurse	die (Kranken)-schwester	(crunken)shvester

operation	die Operation	operats-yohn
optician	der Optiker	opteekair
osteopath	der Knochen-heilkundige	k-nokhen-hilekoondiger
pill	die Tablette	tubletter
(adhesive) plaster	das Pflaster	pflustair
prescription	das Rezept	retsept
X-ray	die Röntgenaufnahme	rerntgen-owfnahmer

Parts of the body

ankle	der Fussknöchel	fooss-knerkhell
arm	der Arm	ahrm
back	der Rücken	ruiken
bladder	die Blase	blahser
blood	das Blut	bloot
body	der Körper	kerpair
bone	der Knochen	k-nokhen
bowels	der Darm	darm
brain	das Gehirn	geheern
breast	die Brust	broost
cheek	die Wange	vunger
chest	die Brust	broost

chin	das Kinn	kin
collar-bone	das Schlüsselbein	shluisselbine
ear	das Ohr	ohr
elbow	der Ellbogen	elbohgen
eye	das Auge	owger
eyelid	das Augenlid	owgenlid
face	das Gesicht	gezikht
finger	der Finger	finger
foot	der Fuss	fōos
forehead	die Stirn	shteern
gums	das Zahnfleisch	zahnfleisch
hand	die Hand	hunt
head	der Kopf	copf
heart	das Herz	hairts
heel	die Ferse	fairzer
hip	die Hüfte	huifter
jaw	der Kiefer	keefer
joint	das Gelenk	gelenk
kidney	die Niere	neerer
knee	das Knie	k-nee
knee-cap	die Kniescheibe	k-neeshiber
leg	das Bein	bine
lip	die Lippe	lipper
liver	die Leber	laybair

lung	die Lunge	lŏŏnger
mouth	der Mund	mŏŏnt
muscle	der Muskel	mŏŏskell
nail	der Nagel	nahgell
neck	der Hals	huls
nerve	der Nerv	nairf
nose	die Nase	nahzer
rib	die Rippe	ripper
shoulder	die Schulter	schŏŏltair
skin	die Haut	howt
stomach	der Magen	mahgen
temple	die Schläfe	shlefer
thigh	der Schenkel	shenkel
throat	der Hals	huls
thumb	der Daumen	dowmen
toe	der Zeh	tsay
tongue	die Zunge	tsŏŏnger
tonsils	die Mandeln	mundeln
tooth	der Zahn	tsahn
vein	die Ader	ahdair
wrist	das Handgelenk	hunt-gelenk

At the dentist's

I must see a dentist	Ich muss zum Zahnarzt
Can I make an appointment?	Kann ich mich anmelden?
As soon as possible, please	Sobald wie möglich bitte
I have toothache	Ich habe Zahnschmerzen
This tooth hurts	Dieser Zahn tut weh
I've lost a filling	Ich habe eine Füllung (Plombe) verloren
Can you fill it?	Können Sie ihn plombieren (füllen)?
Can you do it now?	Können Sie es jetzt machen?
I do not want the tooth taken out	Ziehen Sie den Zahn bitte nicht raus
Please give me an injection first	Bitte geben Sie mir zuerst eine Spritze (örtliche Betäubung)
My gums are swollen/keep bleeding	Mein Zahnfleisch ist geschwollen/blutet immer

I have broken/chipped my dentures	Meine Zahnprotese ist zerbrochen/angeschlagen
Can you fix it (temporarily)?	Können Sie sie (vorläufig) reparieren?
You're hurting me	Sie tun mir weh
How much do I owe you?	Wieviel schulde ich Ihnen?
When should I come again?	Wann soll ich wiederkommen?
Please rinse your mouth	*Bitte spülen Sie den Mund aus
I will X-ray your teeth	*Ich werde Ihre Zähne röntgen
You have an abscess	*Sie haben ein Geschwür (einen Abzess)
The nerve is exposed	*Der Nerv ist blossgelegt
This tooth can't be saved	*Dieser Zahn ist nicht zu retten

Problems and accidents

Where's the police station?	Wo ist die Polizeiwache?
Call the police	Rufen Sie die Polizei
Where is the British consulate?	Wo ist das britische Konsulat?
Please let the consulate know	Bitte benachrichtigen Sie das Konsulat
My bag has been stolen	Man hat mir meine Tasche gestohlen
I found this in the street	Ich habe dies auf der Strasse gefunden
I have lost my luggage/passport/ travellers' cheques	Ich habe mein Gepäck/meinen Pass/meine Reiseschecks verloren
I have missed my train	Ich habe meinen Zug verpasst
My luggage is on board	Mein Gepäck ist an Bord
Call a doctor	Rufen Sie einen Arzt
Call an ambulance	Rufen Sie einen Krankenwagen
There has been an accident	Ein Unfall hat sich ereignet

He's badly hurt	Er ist schwer verletzt
He has fainted	Er ist ohnmächtig geworden
He's losing blood	Er verliert Blut
Please get some water/a blanket/some bandages	Bitte holen Sie etwas Wasser/eine Decke/Verbandszeug
I've broken my glasses	Meine Brille ist kaputt
I can't see	Ich kann nichts sehen
A child has fallen in the water	Ein Kind ist ins Wasser gefallen
A woman is drowning	Eine Frau ist am Ertrinken
May I see your insurance certificate?	*Ich möchte Ihren Versicherungsschein sehen
Apply to the insurance company	*Wenden Sie sich an die Versicherungsgesellschaft
Can you help me?	Können Sie mir helfen?
What are the name and address of the owner?	Wie ist der Name und die Adresse des Besitzers?
Are you willing to act as a witness?	Sind Sie bereit, als Zeuge aufzutreten?
Can I have your name and address, please?	Ihren Namen und Ihre Adresse, bitte
I want a copy of the police report	Ich möchte eine Kopie des Polizeiberichts
There's a bus strike/go slow	*Die Busfahrer sind in den Streik/einen Bummelstreik getreten

Time and dates

TIME

What time is it?	Wie spät ist es?
It's one o'clock	Es ist ein Uhr
two o'clock	zwei Uhr
five past eight[1]	fünf (Minuten) nach acht
quarter past five	Viertel nach fünf
twenty-five past eight	fünf vor halb neun
half past nine	halb zehn
twenty-five to seven	fünf nach halb sieben
twenty to three	zwanzig vor drei
quarter to ten	dreiviertel zehn
Second	die Sekunde
Minute	die Minute
Hour	die Stunde

1. The basic sequence is: five, ten, quarter *past*; ten, five *to half*; half *to next hour*; five, ten *past half*; quarter, ten, five *to next hour*.

It's early/late	Es ist früh/spät
My watch is slow/fast	Meine Uhr geht nach/vor
The clock has stopped	Die Uhr ist stehengeblieben
Sorry I'm late	Entschuldigen Sie die Verspätung

DATE

DATUM

What's the date?	Welches Datum ist heute?
It's December 9th	Es ist der neunte Dezember
We're leaving on January 5th	Wir fahren am fünften Januar ab
We got here on July 27th	Wir sind am siebenundzwanzigsten Juli angekommen

DAY	TAG	tahk
Morning	der Morgen	morgen
this morning	heute Morgen	hoyter morgen
in the morning	am Morgen/ morgens	am morgen/ morgens
Midday, noon	der Mittag	mittahg
at noon	zu Mittag	tsöö mittahg
Afternoon	der Nachmittag	nahkhmittahg
tomorrow afternoon	morgen nachmittag	morgen nahkhmittahg
Evening	der Abend	ahbent

Midnight	Mitternacht	mitter-nukht
Night	die Nacht	nukht
tonight	heute Abend	hoyter ahbent
last night	gestern Abend	gestairn ahbent
Sunrise	der Sonnenaufgang	zonnen-owfgung
Dawn	das Morgengrauen, der Tagesanbruch	morgen-growen/ tahges-anbröökh
Sunset	der Sonnen- untergang	zonnen-ööntairgung
Dusk, twilight	das Zwielicht	tsweelikht
Today	heute	hoyter
Yesterday	gestern	gestairn
two days ago	vorgestern	forgestairn
Tomorrow	morgen	morgen
in two days	übermorgen	uibermorgen
in three days	in drei Tagen	in drī tahgen
WEEK	WOCHE	vohker
Monday	Montag	mohntahg
Tuesday	Dienstag	deenstahg
Wednesday	Mittwoch	mitvokh
Thursday	Donnerstag	donnairstahg
Friday	Freitag	frītahg

Saturday	Samstag/Sonnabend	zumstahg/zonahbent
Sunday	Sonntag	zontahg
on Tuesday	(am) Dienstag	(am) deenstahg
on Sundays	sonntags	zontahgs
Fortnight	zwei Wochen/ vierzehn Tage	tsvi vokhen/feertsayn tahger

MONTH	MONAT	mohnaht
January	Januar	yunōōahr
February	Februar	febrōōahr
March	März	mairts
April	April	upril
May	Mai	mi
June	Juni	yoonee
July	Juli	yoolee
August	August	owgōōst
September	September	Septembair
October	Oktober	Octohbair
November	November	nohvembair
December	Dezember	daytsembair
in March	im März	im mairts

SEASON	JAHRESZEIT	yahres-tsit
Spring	der Frühling, das Frühjahr	fruiling, fruiyahr
Summer	der Sommer	zommair
Autumn	der Herbst	hairbst
Winter	der Winter	vintair
in spring	im Frühjahr	im fruiyahr
during the summer	während des Sommers	vairent des zommers

YEAR	JAHR	yahr
This year	dieses Jahr	deezes yahr
Last year	voriges/vergangenes Jahr	foriges/fairgungenes yahr
Next year	nächstes Jahr	naykhstes yahr

Public holidays

1 January	der Neujahrstag	New Year's Day
6 January	das Dreikönigsfest	Epiphany (Austria only)
	der Karfreitag	Good Friday
	der Ostermontag	Easter Monday
1 May	der Tag der Arbeit	Mayday (not Switzerland)
	der Himmelfahrtstag	Ascension Day
	der Pfingstmontag	Whit Monday
	der Fronleichnam	Corpus Christi (Austria only)
17 June	Siebzehnter Juni	(Germany only)
15 August	Mariä Himmelfahrt	Ascension of the Virgin (Austria only)
1 November	Allerheiligen	All Saints (Austria only)
16 November	Buss- und Bettag	(Germany only)
8 December	die unbefleckte Empfängnis	Conception Day (Austria only)
25 December	der (erste) Weihnachtstag	Christmas Day
26 December	der zweite Weihnachtstag	Boxing Day

Numbers

CARDINAL

0	null	nōōl
1	eins	īnes
2	zwei	tsvī
3	drei	drī
4	vier	feer
5	fünf	fuinf
6	sechs	zekhs
7	sieben	zeeben
8	acht	akht
9	neun	noyn
10	zehn	tsayn
11	elf	elf
12	zwölf	tsverlf
13	dreizehn	drītsayn
14	vierzehn	feertsayn

15	fünfzehn	fuinftsayn
16	sechzehn	zekhtsayn
17	siebzehn	zeebtsayn
18	achtzehn	akhtsayn
19	neunzehn	noyntsayn
20	zwanzig	tsvuntsikh
21	einundzwanzig	in-ōōnt-tsvuntsikh
22	zweiundzwanzig	tsvī-ōōnt-tsvuntsikh
30	dreissig	drīssikh
31	einunddreissig	in-ōōnt-dryssikh
32	zweiunddreissig	tsvy-ōōnt-dryssikh
40	vierzig	feertsikh
41	einundvierzig	ine-ōōnt-feertsikh
50	fünfzig	fuinftsikh
51	einundfünfzig	ine-ōōnt-fuinftsikh
60	sechzig	zekhtsikh
61	einundsechzig	ine-ōōnt-zekhtsikh
70	siebzig	zeebtsikh
71	einundsiebzig	ine-ōōnt-zeebtsikh
80	achtzig	akhtsikh
81	einundachtzig	ine-ōōnt-akhtsikh
90	neunzig	noyntsikh
91	einundneunzig	ine-ōōnt-noyntsikh
100	hundert	hōōndert

101	hunderteins	**hŏŏndertīns**
200	zweihundert	**tsvīhŏŏndert**
1,000	tausend	**towzent**
2,000	zweitausend	**tsvītowzent**
1,000,000	eine Million	**īner meelyohn**

ORDINAL

1st	der erste	**airster**
2nd	zweite	**tsvīter**
3rd	dritte	**dritter**
4th	vierte	**feerter**
5th	fünfte	**fuinfter**
6th	sechste	**zekhster**
7th	siebte	**zeebter**
8th	achte	**akhter**
9th	neunte	**noynter**
10th	zehnte	**tsaynter**
11th	elfte	**elfter**
12th	zwölfte	**tsverlfter**
13th	dreizehnte	**drītsaynter**
14th	vierzehnte	**feertsaynter**
15th	fünfzehnte	**fuinftsaynter**
16th	sechzehnte	**zekhtsaynter**
17th	siebzehnte	**zeebtsaynter**

18th	achtzehnte	**akhtsaynter**
19th	neunzehnte	**noyntsaynter**
20th	zwanzigste	**tsvuntsigster**
21st	einundzwanzigste	**ine-oŏnt-tsvuntsikhster**
30th	dreissigste	**drĭssikhster**
40th	vierzigste	**feertsikhster**
50th	fünfzigste	**fuinftsikhster**
60th	sechzigste	**zekhtsikhster**
70th	siebzigste	**zeebtsikhster**
80th	achtzigste	**akhtsikhster**
90th	neunzigste	**noyntsikhster**
100th	hundertste	**hoŏndertster**
1000th	tausendste	**towzentster**
half	(ein) halb	**halp**
quarter	(ein) Viertel	**feertel**
three quarters	dreiviertel	**drĭfeertel**
a third	ein Drittel	**drittel**
two thirds	zwei Drittel	**tsvī drittel**

Weights and measures

DISTANCE

kilometres – miles

km	*miles or km*	miles	km	*miles or km*	miles
1·6	*1*	0·6	14·5	*9*	5·6
3·2	*2*	1·2	16·1	*10*	6·2
4·8	*3*	1·9	32·2	*20*	12·4
6·4	*4*	2·5	40·2	*25*	15·3
8	*5*	3·1	80·5	*50*	31·1
9·7	*6*	3·7	160·9	*100*	62·1
11·3	*7*	4·4	402·3	*250*	155·3
12·9	*8*	5·0	804·7	*500*	310·7

A rough way to convert from miles to kms: divide by 5 and multiply by 8; from kms to miles divide by 8 and multiply by 5.

LENGTH AND HEIGHT

centimetres – inches

cm	inch or cm	inch		cm	inch or cm	inch
2·5	1	0·4		17·8	7	2·7
5·1	2	0·8		20	8	3·2
7·6	3	1·2		22·9	9	3·5
10·2	4	1·6		25·4	10	3·9
12·7	5	2·0		50·8	20	7·9
15·2	6	2·4		127	50	19·7

A rough way to convert from inches to cm: divide by 2 and multiply by 5; from cm to inches divide by 5 and multiply by 2.

metres – feet

m	ft or m	ft		m	ft or m	ft
0·3	1	3·3		2·4	8	26·3
0·6	2	6·6		2·7	9	29·5
0·9	3	9·8		3	10	32·8
1·2	4	13·1		6·1	20	65·6
1·5	5	16·4		15·2	50	164
1·8	6	19·7		30·5	100	328·1
2·1	7	23		304·8	1,000	3,280

A rough way to convert from ft to m: divide by 10 and multiply by 3; from m to ft divide by 3 and multiply by 10.

metres – yards

m	yds or m	yds		m	yds or m	yds
0·9	1	1·1		7·3	8	8·8
1·8	2	2·2		8·2	9	9·8
2·7	3	3·3		9·1	10	10·9
3·7	4	4·4		18·3	20	21·9
4·6	5	5·5		45·7	50	54·7
5·5	6	6·6		91·4	100	109·4
6·4	7	7·7		457·2	500	546·8

A rough way to convert from yds to m: subtract 10% from the number of yds; from m to yds add 10% to the number of metres.

LIQUID MEASURES

litres – gallons

litres	galls or litres	galls		litres	galls or litres	galls
4·6	1	0·2		36·4	8	1·8
9·1	2	0·4		40·9	9	2·0
13·6	3	0·7		45·5	10	2·2
18·2	4	0·9		90·9	20	4·4
22·7	5	1·1		136·4	30	6·6
27·3	6	1·3		181·8	40	8·8
31·8	7	1·5		227·3	50	11

1 pint = 0·6 litre   1 litre = 1·8 pint

A rough way to convert from galls to litres: divide by 2 and multiply by 9; from litres to galls divide by 9 and multiply by 2.

WEIGHT

kilogrammes – pounds

kg	lb. or kg	lb.	kg	lb. or kg	lb.
0·5	1	2·2	3·2	7	15·4
0·9	2	4·4	3·6	8	17·6
1·4	3	6·6	4·1	9	19·8
1·8	4	8·8	4·5	10	22·1
2·3	5	11·0	9·1	20	44·1
2·7	6	13·2	22·7	50	110·2

A rough way to convert from lb. to kg: divide by 11 and multiply by 5; from kg to lb. divide by 5 and multiply by 11.

grammes	oz.	oz.	grammes
100	3·5	2	57·1
250	8·8	4	114·3
500	17·6	8	228·6
1000 (1 kg)	35	16 (1 lb.)	457·2

TEMPERATURE

centigrade (°C)	fahrenheit (°F)
°C	°F
−10	14
−5	23
0	32
5	41
10	50
15	59
20	68
25	77
30	86
35	95
37	98·4
38	100·5
39	102
40	104
100	180

To convert °F to °C: deduct 32, divide by 9, multiply by 5; to convert °C to °F: divide by 5, multiply by 9 and add 32.

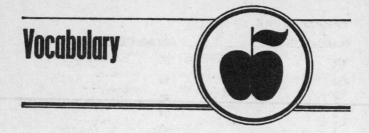

Vocabulary

Various groups of specialized words are given elsewhere in this book and these words are not usually repeated in the vocabulary:

A

a, an	ein/eine/ein	ine/iner/ine
able (to be)	können	kernen
about	ungefähr	ŏŏngefair
above	über	uiber
abroad	im Ausland	im owslunt
accept (to)	annehmen	un-naymen
accident	der Unfall	ŏŏnful
ache (to)	schmerzen	shmairtsen
acquaintance	der Bekannte	bekunter
across	über, jenseits	uiber, yaynzites
act (to)	handeln	hundeln
stage	spielen	shpeelen
add (to)	hinzufügen	hintsŏŏfuigen
address	die Adresse	uddresser
admire (to)	bewundern	bevŏŏndairn
admission	der Eintritt	ine-tritt
advice	der Rat	raht
aeroplane	das Flugzeug	flŏŏktsoyg
afford (to)	sich leisten	zikh listen
afraid	ängstlich	engstlikh
after	nach	nahkh
again	wieder	veedair

against	gegen/wieder	gaygen/veedair
age	das Alter	ulter
agree (to)	zustimmen	tsŏŏshtimmen
ahead	vorn	forn
air	die Luft	lŏŏft
air-conditioning	die Klimaanlage	cleema-unlahger
alike	ähnlich	aynlikh
all	alles	ulles
allow (to)	erlauben	airlowben
all right	in Ordnung	in ordnŏŏng
almost	fast	fust
alone	allein	ullīne
along	entlang	entlung
already	schon	shohn
also	auch	owkh
alter (to)	ändern	endairn
alternative	die Alternative	ultairnahteever
although	obgleich	opglīkh
always	immer	immer
ambulance	der Krankenwagen	crunken-vahgen
America	Amerika	umaireekah
American adj.	amerikanisch	umaireekahnish
noun	der Amerikaner	umaireekahnair
among	zwischen, bei	ts-vishen, bī

amuse (to)	amüsieren	umuizeeren
amusing	amüsant	umuizunt
ancient	sehr alt	zayr ult
and	und	ōōnt
angry	zornig	tsornikh
animal	das Tier	teer
anniversary	die Jahresfeier	yahresfī-er
annoyed	geärgert/verärgert	ge-airgert/fair-airgert
another	ein anderer	ine undairair
answer	die Antwort	untvort
answer (to)	antworten	untvorten
antique	die Antike	unteeker
antique shop	der Antiquitätenladen	unteekveetayten-lahden
any	irgendein	eergent-ine
anyone	irgendeiner	eergent-inair
anything	irgend etwas	eergent etvuss
anyway	jedenfalls	yayden-fuls
anywhere	irgendwo	eergent-voh
apartment	die Wohnung	vohnōōng
apologize (to)	sich entschuldigen	zikh entshōōldigen
appetite	der Appetit	uppeteet
appointment	die Verabredung	fairupraydōōng
architect	der Architekt	urkheetect
architecture	die Architektur	urkheetectōōr

area	das Gebiet	gebeet
arm	der Arm	urm
armchair	der Lehnstuhl	laynshtool
army	das Heer, die Armee	hayr, armay
around	rings herum	rings hairoom
arrange (to)	festsetzen	festzet-tsen
arrival	die Ankunft	unkoonft
arrive (to)	ankommen	uncommen
art	die Kunst	koonst
art gallery	die Kunstgalerie	koonst-galairee
artist	der Künstler	kuinstlair
as	wie	vee
as much as	soviel wie	zohfeel vee
as soon as	sobald	zohbalt
as well/also	auch	owkh
ashtray	der Aschenbecher	ushen-bekher
ask (to)	fragen	frahgen
asleep	eingeschlafen	ine-geshlahfen
at	an/zu/bei/um	un/tsoo/bi/oom
at last	endlich	entlikh
at once	sofort	zohfort
atmosphere	die Atmosphäre	utmohsfairer
attention	die Aufmerksamkeit	owfmairkzumkite
attractive	reizend	rite-sent

auction	die Auktion	owktseeohn
audience	die Zuhörer	tsōōherrer
aunt	die Tante	tunter
Australia	Australien	owstrahleeyen
Australian	australisch	owstrahlish
Austria	Österreich	erstairīkh
Austrian	österreichisch	erstairīkhish
author	der Schriftsteller/	shrift-shtellair/
	Autor	owtor
available	vorhanden	forhunden
average	durchschnittlich	doorkh-shnitlikh
awake	wach	vukh
away	weg	vek
awful	schrecklich	shreklikh

B

baby	das Baby	baybee
bachelor	der Junggeselle	yōōng-gezeler
back	zurück	tsōōruick
bad	schlecht	shlekht
bag	die Tasche	tusher
baggage	das Gepäck	gepeck
bait	der Köder	kerder

balcony	der Balkon	bulkohn
ball *sport*	der Ball	bul
ballet	das Ballet	bulet
band *music*	die Kapelle	cupeller
bank	die Bank	bunk
bare	nackt	nukt
basket	der Korb	corp
bath	das Bad	baht
bathe (to)	baden	bahden
bathing cap	die Bademütze	bahder-muitser
bathing costume	der Badeanzug	bahder-untsöök
bathing trunks	die Badehose	bahder-hohzer
bathroom	das Badezimmer	bahder-tsimmer
battery	die Batterie	butteree
bay	die Bucht	böökht
be (to)	sein	zine
beach	der Strand	shtrunt
beard	der Bart	bahrt
beautiful	schön	shern
because	weil	vile
become (to)	werden	vairden
bed	das Bett	bet
bedroom	das Schlafzimmer	shlahf-tsimmer
before	vor/bevor	for/be-for

begin (to)	beginnen	beginnen
beginning	der Anfang	unfung
behind	hinter	hintair
believe (to)	glauben	glowben
bell	die Glocke	glocker
belong (to)	gehören	geher-ren
below	unter	ŏŏntair
belt	der Gürtel	guirtell
bench	die Bank	bunk
bend (to)	biegen	beegen
beneath	unter	ŏŏntair
berth	das Bett	bet
beside	neben	nayben
besides	ausserdem	owsairdaym
best	das Beste	bester
bet	die Wette	vetter
better	besser	besser
between	zwischen	ts-vishen
bicycle	das Fahrrad	fahrraht
big	gross	grohs
bill	die Rechnung	rekhnŏŏng
binoculars	das Fernglas	fernglahs
bird	der Vogel	fohgell
birthday	der Geburtstag	gebŏŏrtstahg

bite (to)	beissen	bisen
bitter	herb	herp
blanket	die Wolldecke	volldecker
bleed (to)	bluten	blōōten
blind	blind	bleent
blond	blond	blont
blood	das Blut	blōōt
blouse	die Bluse	blōōzer
blow (to)	blasen	blahzen
(on) board	an Bord	un bort
boarding house	die Pension	pensyohn
boat	das Boot, Schiff	boht, sheef
body	der Körper	kerper
bolt	der Türriegel	tuir-reegel
bone	der Knochen	k-nokhen
book	das Buch	bōōkh
book (to)	buchen	bōōkhen
boot	der Stiefel	shteefel
border	die Grenze	grentser
borrow (to)	borgen	borgen
both	beide	bider
bottle	die Flasche	flusher
bottle opener	der Flaschenöffner	flushen-erfnair
bottom	der Boden	boh-den

bowl	die Schüssel	shuisel
box *container*	die Schachtel	shukhtel
theatre	die Loge	lohjer
box office	die Kasse	cusser
boy	der Junge	yŏŏnger
bracelet	das Armband	urmbunt
braces	der Hosenträger	hohzen-trayger
brain	das Gehirn	geheern
branch	der Zweig	ts-vīg
brand	die Marke	murker
brassière	der Büstenhalter	buisten-hultair
break (to)	brechen	brekhen
breakfast	das Frühstück	frui-shtuick
breathe (to)	atmen	ahtmen
bridge	die Brücke	bruicker
briefs	der Schlüpfer	shluipfair
bright	leuchtend/hell	loykhtent/hell
bring (to)	bringen	bringen
British	britisch	british
broken	gebrochen/	gebrokhen/
	zerbrochen	tsair-brokhen
brooch	die Brosche	brosher
brother	der Bruder	brŏŏder
bruise (to)	quetschen	kvetshen

brush	die Bürste	buirster
brush (to)	bürsten	buirsten
bucket	der Eimer	îmer
buckle	die Schnalle	shnuller
build (to)	bauen	bowen
building	das Gebäude	geboyder
bundle	das Bündel	buindel
burn (to)	brennen	brennen
burst (to)	bersten	bairsten
bus	der Bus	bŏŏs
bus stop	die Bushaltestelle	bŏŏs-hulter-shteller
business	das Geschäft	gesheft
busy	beschäftigt	besheftikht
but	aber	ahbair
button	der Knopf	k-nopf
buy (to)	kaufen	cowfen
by	von/bei	fon/bī

C

cabin	die Kabine	cubeener
call *telephone*	der Anruf	unrŏŏf
visit	der Besuch	bezŏŏkh

call (to) *summon*	rufen	rōōfen
name	nennen	nennen
telephone	anrufen	unrōōfen
visit	besuchen	bezōōkhen
calm	ruhig	rōō-eekh
camera	die Kamera/	cumairuh/
	der Fotoapparat	foto-upp-ur-aht
camp (to)	zelten	tselten
camp site	der Zeltplatz	tselt-pluts
can (to be able)	können	kernen
can *tin*	die Dose	dozer
Canada	Kanada	cunahdah
Canadian	kanadisch	cunahdish
cancel (to)	abbestellen	up-beshtellen
candle	die Kerze	kairtser
canoe	das Kanu	kahnoh
cap	die Mütze	muitser
capable	fähig	fayh-eekh
capital city	die Hauptstadt	howpt-shtuht
car	das Auto	owtoh
car park	der Parkplatz	purkpluts
caravan	der Wohnwagen	vohnvahgen
card	die Karte	curter
care (to)	sorgen	zorgen

careful	sorgsam	zorgzahm
careless	unachtsam	ŏŏnukhtzahm
carry (to)	tragen	trahgen
cash	das Bargeld	bahrgelt
cash (to)	einlösen	ine-lerzen
cashier	der Kassierer	cusseerair
casino	das Kasino	cusseenoh
castle	das Schloss/die Burg	shloss/bŏŏrg
cat	die Katze	cutser
catalogue	der Katalog	cutulohg
catch (to)	fangen	fungen
cathedral	der Dom	dohm
catholic	katholisch	cutohleesh
cause	der Grund	groont
cave	die Höhle	herler
central	zentral	tsentrahl
centre	das Zentrum	tsentrŏŏm
century	das Jahrhundert	yahr-hŏŏndairt
ceremony	die Zeremonie	tsayremohnee
certain	sicher	zeekhair
certainly	gewiss	geviss
chair	der Stuhl	shtŏŏl
chambermaid	das Zimmermädchen	tsimmer-maytkhen
chance	die Möglichkeit	mergleekhkite

(by) chance	(durch) Zufall	tsooful
(small) change	das Kleingeld	cline-gelt
change (to)	einwechseln	ine-veckzeln
charge	der Preis	price
charge (to)	berechnen	berekhnen
cheap	billig	billikh
check (to)	nachrechnen	nukh-rekhnen
cheque	der Scheck	sheck
child	das Kind	keent
china	das Porzellan	portselahn
choice	die Wahl	vahl
choose (to)	(aus)wählen	(ows)vaylen
church	die Kirche	keerkher
cigarette case	das Zigarettenetui	tseegahretten-aytvee
cine camera	die Filmkamera	filmcumairuh
cinema	das Kino	keenoh
circus	der Zirkus	tseerkoos
city	die (Gross)stadt	(grohs)shtut
class	die Klasse	clusser
clean	rein	rine
clean (to)	reinigen	rine-eegen
clear	klar	klahr
clerk	der Beamte	beumter
cliff	die Klippe	clipper

climb (to)	besteigen	**besht**īgen
cloakroom	die Toilette	twulette
clock	die Uhr	ōōr
close (to)	schliessen	shleesen
closed	geschlossen	geshlossen
cloth	der Stoff	shtof
clothes	die Kleider	klīdair
cloud	die Wolke	volker
coach	der Autobus	owtohbōōs
coast	die Küste	cuister
coat	der Mantel	muntell
coathanger	der (Kleider)bügel	(klīdair)**buigel**
coin	die Münze	muintser
cold	kalt	cult
collar	der Kragen	crahgen
collar stud	der Kragenknopf	crahgen k-nopf
collect (to)	sammeln	zummeln
colour	die Farbe	furber
comb	der Kamm	cum
come (to)	kommen	commen
come in (to)	hereinkommen	hairīne-commen
comfortable	bequem	bekvaym
common	allgemein	ulgemīne
company	die Gesellschaft	gezelshuft

compartment	das Abteil	uptile
complain (to)	sich beschweren	zikh beshvairen
complaint	die Beschwerde	beshvairder
complete	komplett	komplet
completely	ganz	gunts
concert	das Konzert	contsert
condition	der Zustand	tsooshtunt
conductor *bus*	der Schaffner	shuffnair
orchestra	der Dirigent	deerecgent
congratulations	herzlichen Glückwunsch	hairtsleekhen gluikwŏŏnsh
connect (to)	verbinden	fairbinden
connection *train, etc.*	der Anschluss	unshlŏŏs
consul	der Konsul	conzŏŏl
consulate	das Konsulat	consŏŏlaht
contain (to)	enthalten	enthulten
convenient	günstig	guinstikh
conversation	die Unterhaltung	ŏŏntairhultŏŏng
cook	der Koch, die Köchin	kokh, kerkhin
cook (to)	kochen	kokhen
cool	kühl	kuil
copy	das Exemplar; die Kopie	eksemplahr; kohpee
copy (to)	kopieren	kohpeeyairen

cork	der Korken	corken
corkscrew	der Korkenzieher	corken-tseeyer
corner	die Ecke	ecker
correct	richtig	**reekhtikh**
corridor	der Korridor	correedohr
cosmetics	die Kosmetikartikel	cosmeteek-artikell
cost	der Preis	price
cost (to)	kosten	costen
cotton	die Baumwolle	bowmvoller
cotton wool	die Watte	vutter
couchette	der Liegeplatz	leeger-pluts
count (to)	zählen	tsaylen
country	das Land	lunt
couple	das Paar	pahr
course *dish*	das Gericht	gereekht
courtyard	der Hof	hohf
cousin	der Vetter	fet-air
	die Kusine	cōözeener
cover	die Decke	decker
cover (to)	bedecken	bedecken
cow	die Kuh	koo
crease	die Falte	fulter
credit	das Guthaben	goot-hahben
	der Kredit	kraydeet

crew	die Besatzung	besutsŏŏng
cross	das Kreuz	croyts
cross (to)	hinübergehen	hinuibair-gayen
crossroads	die Kreuzung	croyts-ŏŏng
crowd	die Menge	menger
crowded	voll	fol·
cry (to)	schreien	shri-yen
cufflinks	die Manschetten Knöpfe	munshetten k-nerpfer
cup	die Tasse	tusser
cupboard	der Schrank	shrunk
cure (to)	heilen	hilen
curious	neugierig	noygeerig
curl	die Locke	locker
current	die Strömung	shtrermŏŏng
curtain	der Vorhang	forhung
curve	die Kurve	koorver
cushion	das Kissen	kissen
customs	der Zoll	tsoll
customs officer	der Zollbeamte	tsoll-beumter
cut	der Schnitt	shnit
cut (to)	schneiden	shniden

D

daily	täglich	tayglikh
damaged	beschädigt	beshaydikht
damp	feucht	foykht
dance	der Tanz	tunts
danger	die Gefahr	gefahr
dangerous	gefährlich	gefairlikh
dark	dunkel	dŏŏnkel
date	das Datum	dahtŏŏm
(*appointment*)	die Verabredung	fairupraydŏŏng
daughter	die Tochter	tokhter
day	der Tag	tahg
dead	tot	toht
deaf	taub	towb
dear *expensive*	teuer	toyer
decide (to)	entscheiden	entshīden
deck	das Deck	deck
deckchair	der Liegestuhl	leeger-shtŏŏl
declare (to)	verzollen	fairtsollen
	erklären	airklayren
deep	tief	teef
delay	die Verzögerung	fair-tsergerŏŏng
deliver (to)	austragen	owstrahgen

delivery	die Austragung	owstrahgōōng
demi-pension	das Zimmer mit halber Verpflegung	tsimmer mit hulbair fairpflaygōōng
dentist	der Zahnarzt	tsahnahrtst
deodorant	das desodorierende Mittel/der Deodorant	daysohdoreerender mittel/dayodorunt
depart (to)	abfahren	upfahren
department	die Abteilung	uptīle-ōōng
department store	das Warenhaus	vahrenhows
departure	die Abfahrt	upfahrt
dessert	der Nachtisch	nah-khtish
detour	der Umweg	ōōmvayk
dial (to)	wählen	vaylen
diamond	der Diamant	deeahmunt
dice	der Würfel	vuirfel
dictionary	das Wörterbuch	vertairbōōkh
diet	die Diät	dee-ayt
diet (to)	Diät halten	dee-ayt hulten
different	verschieden	fairsheeden
difficult	schwierig	shveerikh
dine (to)	speisen, essen	spīzen, essen
dining room	der Speisesaal	shpīzerzahl
dinner	das Abendessen	ahbent-essen

direct	direkt	deerekt
direction	die Richtung	reekhtoong
dirty	schmutzig	shmootsikh
disappointed	enttäuscht	ent-toysht
discotheque	Diskothek	diskohtayk
discount	der Preisnachlass	price-nukhluss
dish	die Schüssel	shuisel
disinfectant	das Desinfiziermittel	daysinfeetseermittel
distance	die Entfernung	entfairnoong
disturb (to)	stören	shter-ren
ditch	der Graben	grahben
dive (to)	tauchen	towkhen
diving board	das Sprungbrett	sproongbret
divorced	geschieden	gesheeden
do (to)	tun	toon
dock (to)	anlegen	unlaygen
doctor	der Arzt	ahrtst
dog	der Hund	hoont
doll	die Puppe	pooper
door	die Tür	tuir
double	doppelt	doppelt
double bed	das Doppelbett	doppell-bet
double room	das Doppelzimmer	doppell-tsimmer
down	hinunter	hinoontair

downstairs	unten	ŏŏnten
dozen	das Dutzend	dŏŏtsent
drawer	die Schublade	shŏŏb-lahder
dream	der Traum	trowm
dress	das Kleid	clite
dressing-gown	der Morgenrock	morgenrock
dressmaker	die Damenschneiderin	dahmen-shnĭderin
drink (to)	trinken	treenken
drinking water	das Trinkwasser	treenkvussair
drive (to)	fahren	fahren
driver	der Fahrer	fahrer
drop (to)	fallen lassen	fullen lussen
drunk	betrunken	betrŏŏnken
dry	trocken	trocken
during	während	vayrent

E

each	jeder, e, es	yaydair, yayder, yaydes
early	früh	frui
earrings	die Ohrringe	ohr-ringer
east	der Osten	osten
easy	leicht	likht
eat (to)	essen	essen

edge	der Rand	runt
eiderdown	das Federbett	fayderbet
elastic	das Gummiband	goomeebunt
electric light bulb	die Glühbirne	gluibeerner
electric point	die Steckdose	shteckdoser
electricity	die Elektrizität	aylektreetsitayt
elevator	der Fahrstuhl	fahr-shtool
embarrass (to)	in Verlegenheit setzen	in fairlaygenhite zetsen
embassy	die Botschaft	bohtshuft
emergency exit	der Notausgang	noht-owsgung
empty	leer	layr
end	das Ende	ender
engaged *people*	verlobt	fairlohbt
telephone	besetzt	bezetst
engine	der Motor	mohtor
England	England	englunt
English	englisch	english
Englishman	der Engländer	englendair
enjoy (to)	geniessen	geneessen
enough	genug	genoog
enquiries	die Auskunft	owskoonft
enter (to)	hineintreten	hinine-trayten
entrance	der Eingang	ine-gung

envelope	der (Brief)umschlag	(breef)ōōmshlahg
equipment	die Ausrüstung	ows-ruistōōng
escape (to)	entkommen	entcommen
Europe	Europa	oyrohpah
even *not odd*	gerade	gerahder
event	der Vorfall	forful
ever	immer	immer
every	jeder, e, es	yaydair, yayder, yaydes
everybody	jedermann	yaydairmun
everything	alles	ulles
everywhere	überall	uiberul
example	das Beispiel	bīshpeel
excellent	ausgezeichnet	owsgetsīkhnet
except	ausser	owssair
excess	das Übermass	uibermahss
exchange bureau	die Wechselstube	veckselshtōōber
exchange rate	der Wechselkurs	veckselkoors
excursion	der Ausflug	owsflōōg
excuse	die Entschuldigung	entshōōldeegōōng
exhausted	erschöpft	airsherpft
exhibition	die Ausstellung	owsshtellōōng
exit	der Ausgang	owsgung
expect (to)	erwarten	airvurten
expensive	teuer	toyer

explain (to)	erklären	airklayren
express	die Eilpost	Ile-post
express train	der Schnellzug	shneltsoog
extra	zusätzlich	tsoozetslikh

F

fabric	der Stoff	shtof
face	das Gesicht	gezeekht
face cream	die Gesichtskreme	gezeekhts-craym
face powder	der (Gesichts) Puder	(gezeekhts) poodair
fact	die Tatsache	tahtzukher
factory	die Fabrik	fubreek
fade (to)	verblassen	fairblussen
faint (to)	in Ohnmacht fallen	in ohnmukht fullen
fair	blond	blont
fête	der Jahrmarkt	yahrmurkt
fall (to)	fallen	fullen
family	die Familie	fumeeleeyer
far	weit	vite
fare	das Fahrgeld	fahrgelt
farm	der Bauernhof	bowernhohf
farmer	der Bauer	bower
farther	weiter	vite-air

fashion	die Mode	mohder
fast	schnell	shnell
fat	dick	dick
father	der Vater	fahtair
fault	der Fehler	fayler
fear	die Angst	ungst
feed (to)	ernähren	airnayren
feel (to)	fühlen	fuilen
female *adj.*	weiblich	**vipe-likh**
ferry	die Fähre	fairer
fetch (to)	holen	hohlen
few	wenig	**vaynig**
fiancé(e)	der/die Verlobte	fairlohbter
field	das Feld	felt
fight (to)	kämpfen	**kaimpfen**
fill (to)	füllen	fuilen
film	der Film	film
find (to)	finden	feenden
fine	die Geldstrafe	**gelt-shtrahfer**
finish (to)	vollenden	follenden
finished	fertig	**fairtikh**
fire	das Feuer	foyer
fire escape	der Notausgang	**noht-owsgung**
first	erste	**airster**

first-aid	die erste Hilfe	airster heelfer
first class	die erste Klasse	airster clusser
fish	der Fisch	fish
fish (to)	angeln	ungeln
fisherman	der Fischer	fisher
fishing tackle	die Angelgeräte	ungell-gerayter
fit	fähig	fayh-eekh
fit (to)	passen	pussen
flag	die Fahne	fahner
flat *adj.*	flach	flukh
noun	die Wohnung	vohnoong
flight	der Flug	floog
flippers	Schwimmflossen	shvimflossen
float (to)	obenauf schwimmen	ohbenowf shvimme
flood	die Flut	floot
floor	der Fussboden	fooss-bohden
storey	der Stock	shtock
floor show	das Kabarett	cuburett
flower	die Blume	blöömer
fly	die Fliege	fleeger
fly (to)	fliegen	fleegen
fog	der Nebel	naybel
fold (to)	falten	fulten
follow (to)	folgen	folgen

food	das Essen	essen
foot	der Fuss	fōōs
football	der Fussball	fōōsbul
footpath	der Fussweg	fōōs-vayg
for	für	fuir
foreign	fremd	fremt
forest	der Wald	vult
forget (to)	vergessen	fairgessen
fork	die Gabel	gahbel
forward	vorwärts	forvairts
forward (to)	nachschicken	nukhshicken
fountain	der (Spring)brunnen	(shpring)brōōnen
fragile	zerbrechlich	tsairbrekhlikh
free	frei	frī
freight	die Fracht	frukht
fresh	frisch	frish
fresh water	das Süsswasser	zuis-vussair
friend	der Freund, die Freundin	froynt, froyndin
friendly	freundlich	froyntlikh
from	von	fon
front	die Vorderseite	forderzīter
frontier	die Grenze	grentser
frozen	gefroren	gefrohren

fruit	die Frucht	frookht
full	voll	foll
fun	der Spass	shpahs
funny	komisch	kohmish
fur	der Pelz	pelts
furniture	die Möbel, der Hausrat	merbel, howsraht

G

gallery	die Galerie	gullairee
gamble (to)	(um Geld) spielen	(ŏŏm gelt) shpeelen
game	das Spiel	shpeel
garage	die Garage	gurahjer
garbage	der Abfall	upful
garden	der Garten	gurten
gas	das Gas	gahs
gate	das Tor	tohr
gentlemen	Herren/ Männer	hairren/ mainner
German *adj.*	deutsch	doytsh
noun	der Deutsche	doytsher
Germany	Deutschland	doytshlunt
get (to)	bekommen	becommen

get off (to)	aussteigen	**ows-shtigen**
get on (to)	einsteigen	**ine-shtigen**
gift	das Geschenk	**geshaink**
girdle	der Hüftgürtel	**huift-guirtell**
girl	das Mädchen	**maydkhen**
give (to)	geben	**gayben**
glad	froh	**froh**
glass	das Glas	**glahs**
glasses	die Brille	**breeller**
gloomy	dunkel, schwermütig	**döönkell, shvairmütikh**
glorious	herrlich	**hairlikh**
glove	der Handschuh	**huntshöö**
go (to)	gehen	**gayen**
goal	das Ziel	**tseel**
goal (to score a)	ein Tor schiessen	**tohr sheessen**
god	Gott	**got**
gold	das Gold	**gohlt**
good	gut	**gööt**
government	die Regierung	**regeerööng**
granddaughter	die Enkelin	**enkellin**
grandfather	der Grossvater	**grohs-fahtair**
grandmother	die Grossmutter	**grohs-mööttair**
grandson	der Enkel	**enkel**

grass	das Gras	grahs
grateful	dankbar	dunkbahr
gravel	der Kies	kees
great	gross	grohs
groceries	die Lebensmittel	laybensmittel
ground	der Grund, der Boden	groŏnt, bohden
grow (to)	wachsen	vukhsen
guarantee	die Garantie	guruntee
guard	der Schaffner	shuffnair
guest	der Gast	gust
guide, guide book	der Führer	fuirer

H

hail	der Hagel	hahgel
hair	das Haar	hahr
hair brush	die Haarbürste	hahr-buirster
hairgrip	die Haarklammer	hahrclummer
hairpin	die Haarnadel	hahrnahdell
half	halb	hulp
half fare	der halbe Preis	hulber price
hammer	der Hammer	hummer
hand	die Hand	hunt
handbag	die Handtasche	hunt-tusher

handkerchief	das Taschentuch	tushentōōkh
hang (to)	hängen	haingen
happen (to)	geschehen	geshayen
happy	glücklich	gluiklikh
happy birthday	viel Glück	feel gluik
	zum Geburtstag	tsōōm gebōōrtstahg
harbour	der Hafen	hahfen
hard	hart	hurt
difficult	schwierig	shveerikh
hardly	kaum	kowm
hat	der Hut	hōōt
have (to)	haben	hahben
he	er	air
health	die Gesundheit	gezōōnt-hite
hear (to)	hören	her-ren
heart	das Herz	hairts
heat	die Hitze	hitser
heating	die Heizung	hītsōōng
heavy	schwer	shvair
heel *shoe*	der Absatz	upzuts
height	die Höhe	her-er
help	die Hilfe	heelfer
help (to)	helfen	helfen
hem	der Saum	zowm

her	sie, ihr, ihre	zee, eer, eerer
here	hier	heer
hers	ihr	eer
high	hoch	hohkh
hike (to)	wandern	vundairn
hill	der Hügel, Berg	huigel, bairg
him	ihn, ihm	een, eem
hire (to)	mieten	meeten
his	sein/seine	zine/ziner
hitch hike (to)	per Anhalter fahren	pair unhultair fahren
hold (to)	(fest)halten	(fest)hulten
hole	das Loch	lokh
holiday	der Feiertag	fīyairtahg
holidays	die Ferien	fayree-en
hollow	hohl	hole
(at) home	zu Hause	tsōō howzer
honeymoon	die Hochzeitsreise	hokh-tsaits-rizer
hope	die Hoffnung	hofnōōng
hope (to)	hoffen	hoffen
horse	das Pferd	pfayrt
horse races	das Pferderennen	pfayrder-rennen
horse riding	das (Pferde)reiten	(pfayrde)riten
hospital	das Krankenhaus	crunkenhows
host	der Gastgeber	gastgayber

hostess	die Gastgeberin	gustgayberin
hot	heiss	his
hotel	das Hotel	hohtel
hotel keeper	der Hotelier	hohteleer
hot water bottle	die Wärmflasche	vairmflusher
hour	die Stunde	shtoonder
house	das Haus	hows
how?	wie?	vee
how much, many?	wie viel, wie viele?	vee feel, vee feeler
hungry	hungrig	hoongrikh
hurry (to)	eilen	ilen
hurt (to)	schmerzen/	shmairtsen/
	weh tun	vay toon
husband	der Mann, Gatte	mun, gutter

I

I	ich	eekh
if	wenn	ven
immediately	sofort	sohfort
important	wichtig	veekhtikh
in	in	in
include (to)	einschliessen	ine-shleessen
included	einbegriffen	ine-begriffen

inconvenient	ungelegen	ŏŏngelaygen
incorrect	unrichtig, falsch	ŏŏnreekhtikh, fulsh
indeed	tatsächlich	tahtsekhlikh
indoors	ins Haus	ins hows
information	die Auskunft	owskŏŏnft
information bureau	die Auskunftstelle	owskŏŏnft-ahteller
ink	die Tinte	tinter
inn	das Gasthaus	gusthows
insect	das Insekt	inzekt
insect bite	der Insektenstich	inzekten-shtikh
insect repellant	das Insektenbekämpf-ungsmittel	inzekten-bekempf-ŏŏngs-mittel
inside	drinnen	drinnen
instead of	statt	shtut
instructor	der Lehrer	layrer
insurance	die Versicherung	fair-zeekhairŏŏng
insure (to)	versichern	fair-zeekhairn
interested	interessiert	intairesseert
interesting	interessant	intairessunt
interpreter	der Dolmetscher	dolmetsher
into	in	in
introduce (to)	bekanntmachen	bekunt-mukhen
invitation	die Einladung	ine-lahdŏŏng
invite (to)	einladen	ine-lahden

Ireland	Irland	**eer**-lunt
Irish	irisch	**eer**ish
iron (to)	bügeln, plätten	**buigeln, pletten**
island	die Insel	**eenzell**
it	es	es

J

jacket	die Jacke	yucker
jar	der Krug/Topf	krōōg/topf
jelly fish	die Qualle	kvuller
jewellery	der Schmuck	shmōōck
job	die Stellung	shtellōōng
journey	die Reise	rīzer
jump (to)	springen	shpringen
jumper	der Pullover	pōōlohvair

K

keep (to)	halten, behalten	hulten, behulten
key	der Schlüssel	shlūisel
kick (to)	(mit dem Fuss) stossen	mit dem fōōs shtohsen
kind (friendly)	freundlich	froyntlikh

king	der König	kernikh
kiss	der Kuss	kōōs
kiss (to)	küssen	kuissen
kitchen	die Küche	kuikher
knickers	die Schlüpfer *pl.*	shluipfair
knife	das Messer	messair
knock (to)	klopfen	klopfen
know (to) *fact*	wissen	vissen
person	kennen	kennen

L

label	das Etikett	eteekett
lace	die Spitze	shpitser
ladies	Damen/Frauen	dahmen/frowen
lake	der See	zay
lamp	die Lampe	lumper
land	das Land	lunt
landing	die Landung	lundōōng
landlord/lady	der Hauswirt/wirtin	howsveert/veertin
lane *town*	die Gasse	gusser
country	der Pfad	pfaht
language	die Sprache	shprahkher
large	gross	grohs

last	letzt	letst
late	spät	shpayt
laugh (to)	lachen	lukhen
lavatory	die Toilette	twuletter
lavatory paper	das Toilettenpapier	twuletten pupeer
law	das Gesetz	gezets
lead (to)	führen	fuiren
leaf	das Blatt	blut
leak (to)	auslaufen	owslowfen
learn (to)	lernen	lairnen
least	mindest, wenigst	mindest, vaynikhst
(in the) least	am wenigsten	um vaynikhsten
leather	das Leder	layder
leave (to) *abandon*	verlassen	fairlussen
go away	abfahren	upfahren
(on the) left	links	leenks
left luggage	die Gepäckauf- bewahrung	gepeck-owf- bevahröông
lend (to)	leihen	li-en
length	die Länge	lenger
less	weniger	vaynigair
lesson	der Unterricht	öönter-rikht
let (to) *rent*	vermieten	fairmeeten
allow	erlauben, lassen	airlowben, lussen

letter	der Brief	breef
level crossing	der Bahnübergang	bahnuibergung
library	die Bibliothek	beeblee-ohtayk
licence	die Erlaubnis	airlowbnis
life	das Leben	layben
lift	der Fahrstuhl	fahr-shtool
light *colour*	hell	hell
weight	leicht	likht
noun	das Licht	likht
lighter	das Feuerzeug	foyair-tsoyg
lighter fuel	das Feuerzeug-Benzin	foyairtsoyg-bentseen
lighthouse	der Leuchtturm	loykht-toorm
like (to)	gern haben	gairn hahben
line	die Linie	leenee-yer
linen	das Leinen, die Bettwäsche	linen, betvesher
lingerie	die Unterwäsche	oontervesher
lipstick	der Lippenstift	lippen-shtift
liquid *adj.*	flüssig	fluiseekh
noun	die Flüssigkeit	fluiseekh-kite
listen (to)	zuhören	tsooher-ren
little	klein	kline
live (to)	leben	layben
loaf	das Brot	broht

local	lokal, hiesig, örtlich	lohkahl, heeseekh, ertlikh
lock	das Schloss	shlos
lock (to)	schliessen	shleesen
long	lang	lung
look *at* (to)	ansehen	unzayen
for (to)	suchen	zöökhen
like (to)	aussehen	ows-zayen
loose	los(e)	lohs(er)
lorry	der Lastwagen	lustvahgen
lose (to)	verlieren	fairleeren
lost property office	das Fundbüro	fóónt-buiroh
lot	viel	feel
loud	laut	lowt
love (to)	lieben	leeben
lovely	schön	shern
low	niedrig	needreekh
luggage	das Gepäck	gepeck
(piece of) luggage	das Gepäckstück	gepeckshtuik
lunch	das Mittagessen	meetahgessen

M

mad	verrückt	fair-ruikt
magazine	die Zeitschrift	tsīte-shrift
maid	das (Dienst)mädchen	(deenst)maydkhen
mail	die Post	post
main street	die Hauptstrasse	howptstrahser
make (to)	machen	mukhen
make-up	das Make-up	maykerp
male *adj.*	männlich	menlikh
man	der Mann	mun
manage (to)	auskommen	owscommen
manager	der Leiter	liter
manicure	die Maniküre	muneekuirer
many	viel(e)	feeler
map	die Karte	curter
market	der Markt	murkt
married	verheiratet	fairhīrahtet
Mass	die Messe	messer
massage	die Massage	mussahjer
match	das Streichholz	strīkh-holts
sport	das Spiel	shpeel
material	der Stoff	shtof
matinée	die Matinee	muteenay

mattress	die Matratze	mutruttser
me	mich, mir	meekh, meer
meal	die Mahlzeit	**mahl**tsite
measurements	die Masse	musser
meet (to)	treffen	treffen
mend (to)	reparieren	raypureeren
mess	die Unordnung	öönordnööng
message	die Nachricht	nakh-rikht
metal	das Metall	may**tahl**
middle	die Mitte	mitter
middle aged	in mittlerem Alter	in mitlerem ultair
middle class	die Mittelklasse	mittelclusser
mild	mild	milt
mine *pron.*	mein	mine
minute	die Minute	meenööter
mirror	der Spiegel	**shp**eegel
Miss	Fräulein	**fr**oyline
miss (to)	verpassen	fairpussen
mistake	der Fehler	faylair
mix (to)	(ver)mischen	(fair)**mi**shen
mixed	gemischt	gemisht
modern	modern	moh**dairn**
moment	der Augenblick	owgen-blick
money	das Geld	gelt

month	der Monat	mohnaht
monument	das Denkmal	denkmahl
moon	der Mond	mohnt
more	mehr	mayr
most	meist, die meisten	mist, misten
mother	die Mutter	mŏŏttair
motor boat	das Motorboot	mohtor-boht
motor cycle	das Motorrad	mohtor-raht
motor racing	das Autorennen	owtoh-rennen
motorway	die Autobahn	owtohbahn
mountain	der Berg	bairg
mouthwash	das Mundwasser	mŏŏntvussair
Mr	Herr	hair
Mrs	Frau	frow
much	viel	feel
museum	das Museum	mŏŏzayŏŏm
music	die Musik	mŏŏzeek
must (to have to)	müssen	muissen
my	mein, meine	mine, miner
myself	mich	meekh

N

nail	der Nagel	nahgel
nailbrush	die Nagelbürste	nahgel-buirster
nailfile	die Nagelfeile	nahgel-f1ler
nail polish	der Nagellack	nahgel-luk
name	der Name	nahmer
napkin	die Serviette	zairveeyetter
nappy	die Windel	vindel
narrow	schmal	shmahl
near	in der Nähe von . . .	in dair nayer fon . . .
nearly	fast	fust
necessary	notwendig	nohtvendikh
necklace	die (Hals)kette	(huls)ketter
need (to)	brauchen	browkhen
needle	die Nadel	nahdel
net	das Netz	nets
never	nic, niemals	nee, neemuls
new	neu	noy
news	die Nachrichten	nukh-rikhten
newspaper	die Zeitung	tsītōōng
next	nächst	naikhst
nice	nett	net
night	die Nacht	nukht

nightclub	der Nachtklub	**nukht-clōōb**
nightdress	das Nachthemd	**nukht-hemt**
nobody	niemand	**neemunt**
noisy	lärmend	**lairment**
none	keine, keinen	**kiner, kinen**
north	der Norden	**norden**
not	nicht	**neekht**
(bank) note	der Geldschein	**geltshine**
notebook	das Notizbuch	**nohteets-bōōkh**
nothing	nichts	**neekhts**
notice	die Notiz	**nohteets**
notice (to)	bemerken	**bemairken**
novel	der Roman	**rohmahn**
now	jetzt	**yetst**
number	die Nummer/	**nōōmmer/**
	Zahl	**tsahl**
nylon	das Nylon	**nuilon**
nylons	die Nylonstrümpfe	**nuilon-shtruimpfer**

O

occasion	die Gelegenheit	**gelaygenhite**
occupation	der Beruf	**berōōf**
occupied	besetzt	**bezetst**

ocean	das Meer	mayr
odd *not even*	ungerade	**oo**nger**ah**der
strange	sonderbar	**zon**dairbahr
of	von	fon
off	ab	up
offer	das Angebot	**un**geboht
offer (to)	anbieten	**un**beeten
office	das Büro	buir**oh**
officer, official	der Beamte	be**um**ter
officer *milit.*	der Offizier	offits**eer**
official *adj.*	offiziell	offits**yel**
often	oft	oft
oily	fettig	**fet**tikh
ointment	die Salbe	**zul**ber
old	alt	ult
on	auf, an	owf, un
once	einmal	**ine**-mahl
only	nur	nōōr
open (to)	öffnen	**erf**nen
open *p.p.*	geöffnet	ge-**erf**net
opening	die Öffnung	**erf**nŏŏng
opera	die Oper	**oh**pair
opportunity	die Gelegenheit	gel**ay**gen-hite
opposite	gegenüber liegend	gaygen-**ui**ber leegent

or	oder	ohder
orchestra	das Orchester	orkestair
order (to)	bestellen	beshtellen
ordinary	gewöhnlich	gevernlikh
other	ander	under
otherwise	sonst	zonst
ought	sollen	zollen
our/ours	unser	ŏŏnzer
out	aus	ows
out of order	ausser Betrieb	owssair betreep
outside	draussen	drowsen
over	über	uiber
finished	fertig, zu Ende	fairtikh, tsŏŏ ender
over there	da drüben	dah druiben
overcoat	der Überrock	uiber-rock
overnight	über Nacht	uiber nukht
owe (to)	schulden	shŏŏlden
owner	der Besitzer	bezit-tser

P

pack (to)	packen	pucken
packet	das Paket	puckayt
page	die Seite	ziter

paid	bezahlt	betsahlt
pain	der Schmerz	shmairts
paint (to)	malen	mahlen
painting	das Gemälde	gemaylder
pair	das Paar	pahr
palace	der Palast	pulust
pale	blass	blus
paper	das Papier	pupeer
parcel	das Paket	puckayt
park	der Park	purk
park (to)	parken	purken
part	der Teil	tile
party	die Gesellschaft	gezel-shuft
pass (to)	vorbeigehen	forbī-gayen
passenger	der Passagier	pussujeer
passport	der Pass	pus
past	vorig, früher	forikh, frui-air
path	der Pfad	pfaht
patient	der Patient	putsyent
pavement	der Fussteig	fōōs-shtig
pay (to)	bezahlen	betsahlen
peak	der Gipfel	geepfel
pearl	die Perle	pairler
pebble	der Kiesel	keesel

pedal	das Pedal	pedahl
pedestrian	der Fussgänger	fŏŏsgenger
pen	die Feder	fayder
pencil	der Bleistift	blīshtift
penknife	das Federmesser	fayder-messer
people	die Leute	loyter
perfect	tadellos	tahdel-lohs
per (person)	pro (Person)	pro (pairzohn)
performance	die Aufführung	owf-fuirŏŏng
perfume	das Parfüm	purfuim
perhaps	vielleicht	feelīkht
perishable	leicht verderblich	likht fairdairblikh
permit	die Erlaubnis	airlowbnis
permit (to)	erlauben	airlowben
person	die Person	pairzohn
personal	persönlich	pairzernlikh
petrol	das Benzin	bentseen
petrol station	die Tankstelle	tunk-shteller
petticoat	der Unterrock	ŏŏnter-rock
photograph	die Photographie	phohtoh-grufee
photographer	der Photograph	phohtoh-gruf
piano	das Klavier	cluveer
pick (to)	aussuchen	ows-zŏŏkhen
flowers	pflücken	pfluiken

picnic	das Picknick	peek-neek
piece	das Stück	shtuik
pier	die Landungsbrücke	lundōōngs-bruiker
pillow	das Kopfkissen	kopf-kissen
pin	die Stecknadel	shteck-nahdel
(safety) pin	die Sicherheitsnadel	zeekhairhites-nahdel
pipe	die Pfeife	pfifer
place	der Ort	ort
plain	einfach	ine-fukh
plan	der Plan	plahn
plant	die Pflanze	pfluntser
plastic	plastik	plusteek
plate	der Teller	tellair
platform	der Bahnsteig	bahn-shtig
play	das Schauspiel	show-shpeel
play (to)	spielen	shpeelen
player	der Spieler	shpeeler
please	bitte	bitter
plenty	die Menge	menger
pliers	die Zange *sing.*	tsunger
plug	der Stöpsel	shterpsel
electric	der Stecker	shteckair
pocket	die Tasche	tusher
point	der Punkt	pōōnkt

poisonous	giftig	giftikh
policeman	der Polizist	pohleetsist
police station	die Polizeiwache	pohleetsī-vukher
poor	arm	urm
popular	populär	pohpōōlair
port	der Hafen	hahfen
possible	möglich	merglikh
post (to)	einstecken/aufgeben	īne-shtecken/owf-gayben
post box	der Briefkasten	breef-custen
postcard	die Postkarte	post-curter
postman	der Briefträger	breef-trayger
post office	die Post	post
postpone (to)	zurückstellen	tsōōruikshtellen
pound	das Pfund	pfōōnt
powder	der Puder	pōōdair
prefer (to)	vorziehen	fortseeyen
prepare (to)	vorbereiten	forberiten
present *gift*	das Geschenk	geshaink
press (to)	bügeln, plätten	buigeln, pletten
pretty	hübsch	huipsh
price	der Preis	price
priest	der Priester	preestair
print	der (Ab)druck	(up)drōōck
print (to)	abdrucken	(up)drōōcken

private	privat/	preevaht/
	persönlich	pairzernlikh
problem	das Problem	problaym
profession	der Beruf	berööf
programme	das Programm	prohgrum
promise	das Versprechen	fairshprekhen
promise (to)	versprechen	fairshprekhen
prompt	sofortig	zohfortikh
protestant	der Protestant	protestunt
provide (to)	besorgen	bezorgen
public	öffentlich	erfentlikh
pull (to)	ziehen	tseeyen
pump	die Pumpe	pöömper
pure	rein	rine
purse	das Portemonnaie/	portmonnay/
	die Geldbörse	geltberrser
push (to)	stossen	shtohssen
put (to)	stellen	shtellen
pyjamas	der Schlafanzug	**shlahf**-untsoog

Q

| quality | die Qualität | k-vuleetayt |
| quantity | die Quantität | k-vunteetayt |

quarter	das Viertel	feertel
queen	die Königin	**kern**eegin
question	die Frage	frahger
queue	die Schlange	shlunger
queue (to)	Schlange stehen	shlunger shtayen
quick(ly)	schnell	shnel
quiet(ly)	ruhig	rōō-ikh
quite	ganz	gunts

R

race	das Rennen	rennen
racecourse	die Rennbahn	**renn**bahn
radiator	der Heizkörper	**hīts**-kerper
radio	das Radio	**rah**deeyoh
railway	die Eisenbahn	**īzen**-bahn
rain	der Regen	raygen
rain (to)	regnen	raygnen
raincoat	der Regenmantel	**raygen**-muntel
rare	rar	rahr
rather	ziemlich	tseemlikh
raw	roh	roh
razor	der Rasierapparat	ruzeer upuraht
razor blade	die Rasierklinge	**ruzeer**-clinger

reach (to)	reichen	ríkhen
read (to)	lesen	layzen
ready	bereit	beríte
real	wahr	vahr
really	wirklich	veerklikh
reason	der Grund	gróont
receipt	die Quittung	k-veetóong
receive (to)	bekommen	becommen
recent	neu	noy
recipe	das Rezept	retsept
recognize (to)	erkennen	airkennen
recommend (to)	empfehlen	empfaylen
record	die Schallplatte	shulplutter
record *sport*	der Rekord	record
refreshments	die Erfrischungen	airfrishóongen
refrigerator	der Kühlschrank	cuilshrunk
regards	die Grüsse	gruisser
register (to)	(Gepäck) aufgeben, einschreiben	(gepeck) owfgayben, ine-shríben
relative	der Verwandter, die Verwandte	fairvundtair, fairvundter
religion	die Religion	rayligyohn
remember (to)	sich erinnern	zikh airinnairn
rent	die Miete	meeter
rent (to)	mieten, leihen	meeten, li-en

repair (to)	reparieren	repahreeren
repeat (to)	wiederholen	veederhohlen
reply (to)	antworten	untvorten
reservation	die Reservierung	rezairveeröông
reserve (to)	reservieren	rezairveeren
reserved	reserviert	rezairveert
restaurant	das Restaurant	restorunt
restaurant car	der Speisewagen	shpyzer-vahgen
return (to)	zurückkehren	tsööruik-kairen
return (to) *give back*	zurückgeben	tsööruik-gayben
reward	die Belohnung	belohnôông
ribbon	das Band	bunt
rich	reich	rikh
ride	die Fahrt	fahrt
ride (to)	reiten	riten
right *opp. left*	rechts	rekhts
right *opp. wrong*	richtig	reekhtikh
ring	der Ring	ring
ripe	reif	rife
rise (to)	sich erheben	zikh airhayben
rise (to) *get up*	aufstehen	owfshtayen
river	der Fluss	flôôs
road	die Strasse	strahser
rock	der Felsen	felzen

roll (to)	rollen	rollen
roller *hair*	der Lockenwickler	lockenwiclair
roof	das Dach	dukh
room	das Zimmer	tsimmer
rope	das Seil	zile
rotten	faul	fowl
rough	rauh, grob	row, grohp
round	rund	rŏŏnt
rowing boat	das Ruderboot	rŏŏder-boht
rubber	das Gummi	gŏŏmee
rubbish	der Abfall	upful
rucksack	der Rucksack	rŏŏkzuk
rude	unverschämt	ŏŏnfairshaymt
ruin	die Ruine	rŏŏeener
rule (to)	beherrschen	behairshen
run (to)	laufen	lowfen

S

sad	traurig	trowreekh
safe	sicher	zeekhair
sailor(s)	der Seeman (die Seeleute)	zaymun (zayloyter)
sale *clearance*	der Ausverkauf	owsfairkowf

(for) sale	verkäuflich	fairkoyflikh
salesgirl	die Verkäuferin	fairkoyferin
salesman	der Verkäufer	fairkoyfer
salt water	das Salzwasser	zults-vussair
same	der-, die-, das selbe	zelber
sand	der Sand	zunt
sandal	die Sandale	sundahler
sanitary towel	die Binde	binder
satisfactory	befriedigend	befreedigent
saucer	die Untertasse	ōōntertusser
save (to)	retten	retten
say (to)	sagen	zahgen
scald (to)	verbrühen	fairbruïen
scarf	der Schal	shahl
scenery	die Landschaft	lundshuft
scent	das Parfüm	purfulm
school	die Schule	shōōler
scissors	die Schere	shairer
Scotland	Schottland	shotlunt
Scottish	schottisch	shottish
scratch (to)	kratzen	krutsen
screw	die Schraube	shrowber
screwdriver	der Schraubenzieher	shrowbentsee-er
sculpture	die Skulptur	skōōlptōōr

sea	das Meer/die See	mayr/zay
sea food	die Meeresfrüchte	mayres-fruikhter
seasickness	die Seekrankheit	zay-krunkhite
season	die Jahreszeit	yahres-tsite
seat	der Platz	pluts
second	zweite	ts-viter
see (to)	sehen	zayen
seem (to)	scheinen	shinen
sell (to)	verkaufen	fairkowfen
send (to)	schicken	shicken
separate	getrennt	getrent
serious	ernst	airnst
serve (to)	bedienen	bedeenen
served	serviert	zairveert
service	die Bedienung	bedeenoong
service *church*	der Gottesdienst	gottesdeenst
several	mehrere	mayrerer
sew (to)	nähen	nayen
shade *colour*	der Farbton	furptohn
shade/shadow	der Schatten	shutten
shallow	flach	flukh
shampoo	das Schampoo	shumpoo
shape	die Form	form
share (to)	teilen	tilen

sharp	scharf	shurf
shave (to)	rasieren	rahzeeren
shaving brush	der Rasierpinsel	rahzeer-pinzel
shaving cream	die Rasiercreme	rahzeer-craymer
she	sie	zee
sheet	das Bettlaken	betlahken
shell	die Muschel	mŏŏshell
shelter	das Obdach	opdukh
shine (to)	scheinen	shinen
shingle	der Kiesel	keezel
ship	das Schiff	sheef
shipping line	die Schiff-fahrts-gesellschaft	sheef-fahrts-gezelshuft
shirt	das Hemd	hemt
shock	der Stoss	shtohs
shoe	der Schuh	shŏŏ
shoelace	der Schnürzenkel	shnuir-zenkel
shoe polish	die Schuhwichse	shŏŏvigser
shop	der Laden/	lahden/
	das Geschäft	geshEft
shopping centre	das Einkaufszentrum	ine-kowfs-tsentrŏŏm
shore	das Ufer, die Küste	ŏŏfair, kuister
short	kurz	kŏŏrts
shorts	die Shorts	shorts

show	die Vorstellung	forshtelloong
show (to)	zeigen	tsigen
shower	die Dusche	doosher
shut (to)	schliessen	shleesen
shut *p.p.*	geschlossen	geshlossen
side	die Seite	ziter
sights	die Sehenswürdig- keiten	sayens-vuirdikh-kiten
sightseeing	die Besichtigung von Sehenswürdig- keiten	bezikhtigoong von sayens-vuirdikh- kiten
sign	das Zeichen	tsikhen
sign (to)	unterschreiben	oontair-shriben
signpost	der Wegweiser	**vayk-vizer**
silver	das Silber	zilbair
simple	einfach	ine-fukh
since	seit	zite
sing (to)	singen	zingen
single	einzig, einzeln	ine-tsig, ine-tseln
single room	das Einzelzimmer	ine-tsel-tsimmer
sister	die Schwester	shvester
sit (to)	sitzen	zitsen
sit down (to)	sich setzen	zikh zetsen
size	die Grösse	grerser

skating	das Schlittschuh-laufen	shlitshōō-lowfen
skid (to)	rutschen	rōōtshen
skiing	das Skilaufen	shee-lowfen
skirt	der Rock	rock
sky	der Himmel	himmel
sleep (to)	schlafen	shlahfen
sleeper	der Schlafwagen	shlahf-vahgen
sleeping bag	der Schlafsack	shlahf-zuck
sleeve	der Ärmel	airmel
slice	die Schnitte	shnitter
slip	der Unterrock	ōōnter-rock
slipper	der Hausschuh	hows-shōō
slowly	langsam	lungzum
small	klein	kline
smart	schick	shick
smell	der Geruch	gerōōkh
smell (to)	riechen	reekhen
smile (to)	lächeln	lekheln
smoke (to)	rauchen	rowkhen
smoking compartment	Raucher	rowkhair
(no) smoking	rauchen (verboten)	rowkhen fairbohten
snow	der Schnee	shnay

snow (to)	schneien	shni-yen
so	so	zoh
soap	die Seife	zifer
soap powder	das Seifenpulver	zífenpōolfair
sober	nüchtern	nuíkhtairn
sock	die Socke	zocker
soft	weich	víkh
sold	verkauft	fairkowft
sole *shoe*	die Sohle	zohler
solid	fest	fest
some	einige, etwas	íneeger, etvus
somebody	jemand	yaymunt
somehow	irgendwie	eergentvee
something	etwas	etvus
sometimes	manchmal	munkhmahl
somewhere	irgendwo	eergentvoh
son	der Sohn	zohn
song	das Lied	leet
soon	bald	bult
sort	die Art	ahrt
sound	der Laut	lowt
sour	sauer	zower
south	der Süden	zuiden
souvenir	das Andenken	undenken

space	der Raum	rowm
spanner	der Schrauben- schlüssel	shrowben-shluissel
spare	Ersatz-, Reserve-	airzats, rezairver
speak (to)	sprechen	shprekhen
speciality	die Spezialität	shpaytseeyulitayt
spectacles	die Brille *sing.*	briller
speed	die Geschwindigkeit	geshvindikh-kite
speed limit	die Geschwindigs- grenze	geshvindikhs-grentser
spend (to)	ausgeben	owsgayben
spoon	der Löffel	lerffel
sport	der Sport	shport
sprain (to)	verstauchen	fairshtowkhen
spring *water*	die Quelle	kveller
square	viereckig	feer-eckikh
square metre	das Quadratmeter	kvudrahtmaytair
square *noun*	der Platz	pluts
stable	der Stall	shtul
stage	die Bühne	buiner
stain	der Fleck	fleck
stained	beschmutzt	beshmöötst
stairs	die Treppe	trepper
stale	schal	shahl
stalls	der Sperrsitz	shpair-zits

stamp	die Briefmarke	breefmurker
stand (to)	stehen	shtayen
star	der Stern	shtairn
start (to)	anfangen	unfungen
(main) station	der (Haupt)bahnhof	(howpt)bahnhohf
statue	die Bildsäule	beelt-zoyler
stay (to)	bleiben	blíben
step	der Schritt	shrit
steward	der Steward	shtōō-urt
stewardess	die Stewardess	shtōō-urdess
stick	der Stock	shtock
stiff	starr	shtur
still *not moving*	still	shtil
still *time*	noch	nokh
sting	der Stich	steekh
stocking	der Strumpf	shtrōōmpf
stolen	gestohlen	geshtohlen
stone	der Stein	shtíne
stool	der Stuhl, Hocker	shtōōl, hockair
stop (to)	(an)halten	(un)hulten
storm	der Sturm	shtōōrm
stove	der Ofen	ohfen
straight	gerade	gerahder
straight on	gerade aus	gerahder ows

strange	sonderbar	zondairbahr
strap	der Riemen	reemen
stream	der Bach	bukh
street	die Strasse	strahser
stretch (to)	(aus)strecken	(ows)shtrecken
string	die Schnur	shnōōr
strong	stark	shturk
student	der Student	shtōōdent
stung (to be)	gestochen werden	geshtokhen vairden
style	der Stil	shteel
suburb	der Vorort	forort
subway	die Unterführung	ōōnterfuirōōng
such	solch	solkh
suede	das Wildleder	vilt-laydair
sugar	der Zucker	tsōōcker
suggestion	der Vorschlag	forshlahg
suit *men*	der Anzug	untsōōg
suit *women*	das Kostüm	costuim
suitcase	der (Hand)koffer	(hunt)coffer
sun	die Sonne	zonner
sunbathe (to)	sonnenbaden	zonnen-bahden
sunburn	der Sonnenbrand	zonnen-brunt
sunglasses	die Sonnenbrille	zonnen-briller
sunhat	der Sonnenhut	zonnen-hōōt

sunny	sonnig	**zonnikh**
sunshade	der Sonnenschirm	**zonnen-sheerm**
suntan oil	das Sonnenöl	**zonnen-erl**
supper	das Abendessen	**ahbent-essen**
sure	sicher	**zeekher**
surgery	das Sprechzimmer	**shprekh-tsimmer**
surgery hours	die Sprechstunde	**shprekh-stöönder**
surprise	die Überraschung	**uibair-rushööng**
surprise (to)	überraschen	**uibair-rushen**
suspender belt	der Strumpfgürtel	**shtröömpf-guirtel**
sweater	der Pullover	**pöölohvair**
sweet	süss	**zuis**
sweets	die Bonbons	**bonbons**
swell (to)	anschwellen	**unshvellen**
swim (to)	schwimmen	**shvimmen**
swimming pool	die Badeanstalt	**bahder-unstult**
swings	die Schaukel, die Wippe	**showkel, vipper**
Swiss	schweizerisch	**shvītserish**
switch *elec.*	der (Licht)schalter	**(likht)shultair**
Switzerland	Schweiz	**shvīts**
swollen	angeschwollen	**ungeshvollen**
synagogue	die Synagoge	**zuinagohger**

T

table	der Tisch	tish
tablecloth	das Tischtuch	tishtookh
tablet	die Tablette	tubletter
tailor	der Schneider	shnidair
take (to)	nehmen	naymen
talk (to)	reden	rayden
tall	gross	grohs
tank	der Tank	tunk
tanned	sonnverbrannt	zonfairbrunt
tap	der Wasserhahn	vussair-hahn
taste	schmecken	shmecken
tax	die (Kur)taxe	(coor)-tukser
taxi	das Taxi	tuksee
taxi rank	der Taxistand	tuksee-shtunt
teach (to)	lehren	layren
tear	der Riss	ris
tear (to)	(zer)reissen	(tsair)rissen
teaspoon	der Teelöffel	tay-lerffel
telegram	das Telegramm	taylegrum
telephone	das Telefon	taylefohn
telephone (to)	telefonieren	taylefohneeren
telephone box	die Telefonzelle	taylefohn-tseller

telephone call	der Anruf	unrōōf
telephone directory	das Telefonbuch	taylefohn-bōōkh
telephone number	die Telefonnummer	taylefohn-nōōmmair
telephone operator	das Telefonfräulein	taylefohn-froyline
television	das Fernsehen	fairnzayen
tell (to)	erzählen	airtsaylen
temperature	die Temperatur	tempairutōōr
temple	der Tempel	tempel
temporary	vorläufig,	forloyfeekh,
	vorübergehend	foruibairgayent
tennis	das Tennis	tennis
tent	das Zelt	tselt
tent peg	der Zeltpflock	tselt-pflock
tent pole	der Zeltmast	tseltmust
terrace	die Terrasse	tairrusser
than	als	uls
that	jener, e, es	yaynair, yayner,
		yaynes
the	der, die, das	dair, dee, dus
theatre	das Theater	tayahtair
their(s)	ihr, ihre	eer, eerer
them	sie, ihnen	zee, eenen
then	dann	dun
there	da, dort	dah, dort

there is	es ist/gibt	es eest/geebt
there are	es sind/gibt	es zint/geebt
thermometer	das Thermometer	tairmohmaytair
these	diese	deezer
they	sie	zee
thick	dick	dick
thin	dünn	duin
thing	das Ding, die Sache	ding, zukher
think (to)	denken	denken
thirsty	durstig	doorstikh
this	dieser, e, es	deezair, deezer, deezes
those	jene	yayner
though	obwohl	opvohl
thread	der Faden	fahden
through	durch	doorkh
throughout	während	vairent
throw (to)	werfen	vairfen
thunderstorm	das Gewitter	gevittair
ticket	die Karte	curter
tide	die Gezeiten (*pl.*)	getsiten
tie	der Schlips	shlips
tie *sport*	der Gleichstand	glikh-shtunt
tight	eng	eng
time	die Zeit	tsit

timetable	der Fahrplan	**fahrplahn**
tin	die Dose	dohzer
tin opener	der Dosenöffner	**dohzen**-erfnair
tip	das Trinkgeld	**trinkgelt**
tip (to)	ein Trinkgeld geben	ine **trinkgelt** gayben
tired	müde	muider
tissues	die Papiertücher	pupeer-tuikhair
to	zu, nach	tsōō, nukh
tobacco	der Tabak	tubuck
tobacco pouch	der Tabaksbeutel	tubucksboytel
together	zusammen	tsōōzummen
toilet	die Toilette	twuletter
toilet paper	das Toilettenpapier	twulettenpupeer
too *also*	auch	owkh
too (much, many)	zu (viel, viele)	tsōō (feel, feeler)
toothbrush	die Zahnbürste	**tsahn**-buirster
toothpaste	die Zahnpasta	**tsahn**-pustu
toothpick	der Zahnstocher	**tsahn**-shtokhair
top	das obere Ende	**ohbairer** ender
torch	die Taschenlampe	**tushen**-lumper
torn	zerrissen	tsairrissen
touch (to)	berühren	beruiren
tough	hart, zäh	hurt, tsay
tour	die (Rund)reise	(rōōnt)rizer

tourist	der Tourist	tŏŏreest
towards	gegen	gay-gen
towel	das Handtuch	hunt-tŏŏkh
tower	der Turm	tŏŏrm
town	die Stadt	shtut
town hall	das Rathaus	rahthows
toy	das Spielzeug	shpeel-tsoyg
traffic	der Verkehr	fairkayr
traffic jam	die Verkehrsstockung	fairkayrs-shtockŏŏng
traffic lights	die Verkehrsampel	fairkairs-umpell
trailer	der Anhänger	unhenger
train	der Zug	tsŏŏg
tram	die Strassenbahn, S-bahn	shtrahsenbahn, es-bahn
transfer (to)	übertragen	uibertrahgen
transfer (to) *travel*	umbuchen	ŏŏmbŏŏkhen
transit	der Durchgang	dŏŏrkhgang
translate (to)	übersetzen	uiber-zetsen
travel (to)	reisen	rizen
travel agency	das Reisebüro	rizer-buiroh
traveller	der Reisende	rizendair
traveller's cheque	der Reisescheck	rize-sheck
treat (to)	behandeln	behundeln
treatment	die Behandlung	behuntlŏŏng

tree	der Baum	bowm
trip	der Ausflug	owsflōōg
trouble	die Mühe	mui-er
trousers	die Hose *sing.*	hohzer
true	wahr	vahr
trunk	der Koffer	coffair
trunks *swimming*	die Badehose	bahder-hohzer
truth	die Wahrheit	vahrhīte
try (to)	versuchen	fairzōōkhen
try on (to)	anprobieren	unprohbeeren
tunnel	der Tunnel	tōōnel
turn (to)	umdrehen	ōōmdrayen
turning	die Biegung	beegōōng
tweezers	die Pinzette *sing.*	pintsetter
twin-bedded room	das Zweibettzimmer	tsvībet-tsimmer
twisted	verrenkt	fairrenkt

U

ugly	hässlich	heslikh
umbrella	der Regenschirm	raygensheerm
(beach) umbrella	der Sonnenschirm	zonnensheerm
uncle	der Onkel	onkel
uncomfortable	unbequem	ōōnbekvaym

under(neath)	unter	ŏŏntair
underground	die U-bahn	ŏŏ-bahn
understand (to)	verstehen	fairshtayen
underwater fishing	die Unterwasser-fischerei	ŏŏntairvusserfisher-ī
underwear	die Unterwäsche	ŏŏntair-vesher
university	die Universität	ŏŏneevairseetayt
unpack (to)	auspacken	owspucken
until	bis	bis
unusual	ungewöhnlich	ŏŏngevernlikh
up	auf	owf
upstairs	oben	ohben
urgent	dringend	dringent
us	uns	ŏŏns
U.S.A.	die Vereinigten Staaten	fairīnigter shtahten
use (to)	brauchen	browkhen
useful	brauchbar	**browkh**bahr
useless	unbrauchbar	ŏŏnbrowkhbahr
usual	gewöhnlich	gevernlikh

V

vacancies	Zimmer frei	tsimmer fri
vacant	frei	fri
vacation	die Ferien	faireeyen
valid	gültig	guiltikh
valley	das Tal	tahl
valuable	wertvoll	vairtfol
value	der Wert	vairt
vase	die Vase	vahzer
vegetable	das Gemüse	gemuiner
vegetarian	der Vegetarier	fegetahree-er
ventilation	die Ventilation	ventilahtsyohn
very	sehr	zayr
very much	viel, sehr	feel, zayr
vest	das Unterhemd	õontairhemt
view	der Blick	blik
villa	das Villa	veelah
village	das Dorf	dorf
violin	die Geige	giger
visa	das Visum	veezõom
visibility	die Sicht(barkeit)	sikhtbahrkite
visit	der Besuch	bezõokh
visit (to)	besuchen	bezõokhen

voice	die Stimme	shtimmer
voltage	die Spannung	shpunnõong
voyage	die Reise	rizer

W

wait (to)	warten	vurten
waiter	der Kellner	kelnair
waiting room	der Warteraum	vurter-rowm
waitress	die Kellnerin	kelnerin
wake (to)	aufwachen	owf-vukhen
Wales	Wales	vayls
walk	der Spaziergang	shputseer-gung
walk (to)	spazierengehen	shputseeren-gayen
wall *inside*	die Wand	vunt
wall *outside*	die Mauer	mowair
wall plug	der Stecker	shteckair
wallet	die Brieftasche	breef-tusher
want (to)	wollen	vollen
wardrobe	der Kleiderschrank	klider-shrunk
warm	warm	vurm
wash (to)	waschen	vushen
washbasin	das Waschbecken	vush-becken
waste	der Abfall	upful

waste (to)	verschwenden	fairshvenden
watch	die Armbanduhr	urmbunt-ōōr
water	das Wasser	vussair
waterfall	der Wasserfall	vussairful
water skiing	das Wasserskilaufen	vussair-shee-lowfen
waterproof	wasserdicht	vussairdikht
wave	die Welle	veller
way	der Weg	vayg
we	wir	veer
wear (to)	tragen	trahgen
weather	das Wetter	vetter
week	die Woche	vokher
weigh (to)	wiegen	veegen
weight	das Gewicht	geveekht
welcome	willkommen	vilcommen
well	gut	gōōt
Welsh	walisisch	vuleezish
west	der Westen	vesten
wet	nass	nus
what?	was?	vus
wheel	das Rad	raht
when?	wann?	vun
where?	wo?	voh
whether	ob	op

which?	welcher, e, es?	velkhair, velkher, velkhes
while	während	vairent
who?	wer?	vair
whole	ganz	gunts
whose?	wessen?	vessen
why?	warum?	vahrōōm
wide	weit	vīte
widow	die Witwe	veetver
widower	der Witwer	veetvair
wife	die Frau	frow
wild	wild	vilt
win (to)	gewinnen	gevinnen
wind	der Wind	vint
window	das Fenster	fenstair
wing	der Flügel	fluigel
wire	der Draht	draht
wish (to)	wünschen	vuinshen
with	mit	mit
without	ohne	ohner
woman	die Frau	frow
wood	der Wald	valt
wood *timber*	das Holz	holts
wool	die Wolle	voller

word	das Wort	vort
work	die Arbeit	**ar**bite
work (to)	arbeiten	**ar**biten
worry (to)	(sich) beunruhigen	(zikh) beoŏnroō-eegen
worse	schlechter	shlekhtair
worth (to be)	wert sein	vairt zine
wrap (to)	wickeln	vickeln
write (to)	schreiben	shrĭben
writing paper	das Schreibpapier	**shrĭp-**pupeer
wrong	falsch	fulsh

Y

yacht	die Jacht	yukht
year	das Jahr	yahr
yet	noch	nokh
you	Sie/du (familiar)	zee/doō
young	jung	yŏŏng
your	Ihr, dein	eer, dĭne
youth hostel	die Jugendherberge	**yoo**gent-hair-bairger

Z

| zip | der Reissverschluss | rĭce-fairshloōss |
| zoo | der Zoo | tsoh |

Index

A History of
Capitalism
According to
The Jubilee Line

John O'Farrell

A Political Short Story

PENGUIN BOOKS

PENGUIN BOOKS

Published by the Penguin Group
Penguin Books Ltd, 80 Strand, London WC2R ORL, England
Penguin Group (USA) Inc., 375 Hudson Street, New York, New York 10014, USA
Penguin Group (Canada), 90 Eglinton Avenue East, Suite 700, Toronto, Ontario,
Canada M4P 2Y3 (a division of Pearson Penguin Canada Inc.)
Penguin Ireland, 25 St Stephen's Green, Dublin 2, Ireland (a division of Penguin Books Ltd)
Penguin Group (Australia), 707 Collins Street, Melbourne, Victoria 3008, Australia
(a division of Pearson Australia Group Pty Ltd)
Penguin Books India Pvt Ltd, 11 Community Centre, Panchsheel Park, New Delhi – 110 017, India
Penguin Group (NZ), 67 Apollo Drive, Rosedale, Auckland 0632, New Zealand
(a division of Pearson New Zealand Ltd)
Penguin Books (South Africa) (Pty) Ltd, Block D, Rosebank Office Park, 181 Jan Smuts Avenue,
Parktown North, Gauteng 2193, South Africa

Penguin Books Ltd, Registered Offices: 80 Strand, London WC2R ORL, England

www.penguin.com

First published in Penguin Books 2013
001

Copyright © John O'Farrell, 2013
All rights reserved

The moral right of the author has been asserted

Set in 11.75/15pt Baskerville MT Std
Typeset by Jouve (UK), Milton Keynes
Printed in England by Clays Ltd, St Ives plc

ISBN: 978-1-846-14634-3

www.greenpenguin.co.uk

ALWAYS LEARNING   PEARSON

I

'This is Jubilee Line information. We would like to apologize for the inconvenience while we are being held in the tunnel. This is due to a crisis in capitalism. We're just waiting for a green light and hope to be on our way again as soon as the owners of the means of production, distribution and exchange have resolved the inherent contradictions in dialectical materialism.'

Sometimes you hear people say, 'Oh, I had a nightmare journey on the tube,' and you understand that their commute home on the London Underground was more unpleasant than usual. We don't take the word 'nightmare' to mean that in the middle of a packed carriage they literally realized that they were wearing their pyjamas and then felt their teeth crumbling as their childhood maths teacher stood before them pointing and laughing, only it wasn't exactly the tube because it was also the kitchen.

Well, I *literally* dreamt the journey to hell on the London Underground. I fell asleep on the Jubilee Line and the remainder of my journey could not have been more unreal if a group of teenagers had been content with their original choice of carriage.

'I had a nightmare on the tube this morning,' I said to my wife that night, as if to test my point.

'Hmm . . .' she mumbled, barely looking up from the television. 'Me too. "Customer under a train at Baker Street . . ."' and she chuckled at a funny advertisement.

'Did they really say "customer"?' I asked her. 'Was that all that defined him in his final moments? Someone who "consumed", someone who purchased something? The buyer of one measly tube ticket?'

'What?'

She picked up the remote and paused the TV until I had finished talking.

'If they are going to try and sum you up in a single word, you'd want your epitaph to say a bit more about you than the fact that you were a "customer" of London Transport. "Competent bass guitarist under a train at Baker Street," maybe. Or "Banker under a train at Baker Street".'

'They couldn't say that,' she said, pressing 'play' on the TV remote. 'There'd be too much of a cheer on the platform.'

'This is Jubilee Line information again. We apologize once more for the delay on this train, which we understand is due to a sudden and total collapse in the social, political and economic system above ground since we commenced this journey. Apparently efforts are being made to resolve the situation as quickly as possible and we hope to be on our way as soon as a new way of organizing twenty-first-century society has been resolved.'

That was how it had begun. On this day as so often before, I had boarded the train at its source in the foothills of suburbia. The quiet, unassuming station of Stanmore is an overground Underground station in the middle of nowhere; a terminus straight from the 1930s and about as radical and exciting as a wireless broadcast by Stanley Baldwin. I always liked to stare out the window, watching the suburbs turn into city, until eventually the train disappeared under the metropolis after Finchley Road.

A place generally turns its worst side to its railway lines. It is the part of any town that is observed by more passers-by than any other, yet the great municipalities seem to have decided that the way to showcase their most popular views is to cover them with brambles and rotting grass cuttings and abandoned bicycles with bindweed weaving its way through the rusty spokes. If they're feeling really extravagant they will treat the casual observer to a display of traditional local cabling. On this bleak section, cable-spotters will be thrilled to see miles and miles of cables of different fading colours arranged in sagging rows, one above the other. In one or two places there are cable *arches*, glorious monuments to the triumph of cabling through which trains may ceremoniously pass.

From Stanmore, the Jubilee Line passes through a series of unremarkable suburbs such as Canons Park and Kingsbury. The train pauses for forty-five seconds in these places, which frankly is more than enough. Most exciting of all the early stops is the historic jewel that is Queensbury. Unlike, say, Rome, Jerusalem or Alexandria, Queensbury rather lacks a world-changing narrative stretching back through the millennia. Basically, in 1932 they put a tube stop in the middle of a field and had to give it a name.

'Where are we putting this station?'

'Nowhere, sir.'

'Nowhere – what are you talking about?'

'Well, once the place has an Underground station, the plan is to sell off the land for housing and shops or whatever. But at the moment, it's just a field. So we have to find a suitable name . . .'

'OK. Look, it's half past five on a Friday afternoon. What's the next station along the line called?'

'Kingsbury, sir.'

'Okay. This one's called Queensbury. Was there anything else?'

Now, there are people who were born in Queensbury, there is a song about Queensbury, there are Queensbury ward councillors, there are proud Queensburgians who may or may not take pride in their rich heritage and its roots in the back office of the Metropolitan Railway Company.

Perhaps it had been thinking about these nondescript suburbs that had caused me to drift off. But at some point soon after the Jubilee Line disappeared underground, I was rocked into a deep, deep sleep. Now the journey was through my subconscious: I passed straight from Zone 3 to Zone ∞.

In my dream the train came to an abrupt halt

in a tunnel and it became clear that this was no ordinary delay. According to the oracle, there had been some sort of economic meltdown that had shut down *everything*. I don't know how I knew this, but I understood that the power that drove the trains had suddenly cut out; that in the minutes since I had swiped my Oyster card at Stanmore, London Transport had gone bankrupt and been dissolved but with no one taking over responsibility for their system. Because everything else had frozen too, the house of cards had all come crashing down as some analysts had been warning it would for some time.

'Oh, for goodness' sake,' said an irritated woman sitting opposite me. 'They've always got some bloody excuse, haven't they?'

'Yeah . . .' said a portly man in a T-shirt. 'Although as excuses go, the total collapse of capitalism is quite a big one.'

I knew that this was no ordinary delay because people on the London Underground had actually started talking to one another. That never happens unless something really

astonishing has occurred. After the Blitz
began in September 1940, Londoners dashed
to take cover in the tube stations. Apparently
it was not until June 1944 and the fall of the
first doodlebug that someone finally broke
the awkward silence by tutting and muttering,
'Honestly, this is a bit much, isn't it?'

Now the crisis on the news had impacted on
our own lives, in a way that we had somehow
presumed it never really would. It was just so
hard to understand what the doom-mongers
were trying to explain that nobody really took
it in. At least during the Blitz the concept
of bombs being dropped from the sky was
something everyone could instantly grasp. But
this disaster was all the more sinister because
it defied comprehension. We were all in great
danger from that most dangerous of threats:
a boring one. Like the venomous snake that
sedates its prey before swallowing it, the dull
complexity of twenty-first-century capitalism
numbed its victims into confused submission
before swallowing them whole.

We had all taken it for granted that trains went along their tracks, that the Internet worked, and that food arrived in the supermarkets and cash came out of the dispensers to pay for it all. But it all depended on the flow of money between institutions, on software programs that could not authorize unlimited debits without the requisite incoming flow of capital. Money was the electricity that made everything move. And then all the fuses had blown.

And so our train was stuck in a tunnel, because presumably there was no supply of electricity being authorized to transport the train. We still had lights in the carriage and the tannoy clearly still worked, even if in retrospect it was a little strange that they had recorded messages specifically for this bizarre and complex set of circumstances.

'This is Jubilee Line information. We apologize once again for the complex chain of events that has immobilized the entire Western economy, its systems and infrastructure. Customers are advised that they may need to reconstruct twenty-first-century society along nomadic

hunter-gatherer principles, replacing the representative
money tokens with a primitive system of bartering. In
the meantime, may we remind you to take any belongings
with you when leaving the train.'

'Oh yeah,' I said, 'don't forget to take your
bloody umbrella. Because you might be able
to swap it for an ox.' And there were a few
half-nods of outraged agreement in the row
opposite.

'Please?' said a strong foreign accent, and
I looked up to see a smartly dressed woman
looking a little confused. 'This train? Stratford?'

'Hopefully!' I replied with a smile. 'They're
having a few technical difficulties . . .'

'Please?'

'Er – delay? Wait here?'

She looked Turkish, or Lebanese, perhaps.
In any case, the speaker of a language in which
any attempt to use the French word and put an
'o' on the end would not get me any further.

'Everything's buggered, me darlin'!'
said a large man in an England shirt, but

unsurprisingly she didn't nod and go, 'Oooh, "buggered", thank you!'

For the rest of us, despite the various warnings that this day had always been going to come, there was an air of incredulity in our carriage. The increasingly alarming economic news in the previous few months meant that we knew this wasn't just some elaborate hoax for a hidden-camera TV show. It would have been a pretty determined Noel Edmonds to arrange for the global news networks to spend months predicting society's collapse just so the dozen of us in this carriage wouldn't suspect anything when he sprang this particular 'Gotcha!'

As tends to be the case with dreams, there were many presumptions and false normalities that everyone just accepted. On this tube train men were sitting with their legs together. No one was eating a smelly McDonald's meal. And all of us accepted this as completely natural. But after many minutes stuck in a tunnel, the cast of characters in this carriage began to get edgy.

'Why isn't the driver telling us what to do?' said the cross woman, who seemed to be with the man in the England shirt.

'There is no driver on this line now,' said the man whose stomach would have already advertised an interest in beer without the Real Ale T-shirt.

'He's right,' added an elderly, academic-looking man. 'Remember the whole "Driverless Trains" debate during the last mayoral election?'

'No?'

'Boris Johnson was attacked for planning to extend them, but still won.'

'Was he?' said the woman. 'I must have missed that. I just voted for Boris 'cos he was funny on *Have I Got News for You*.'

None of us could quite come to terms with the notion that we were completely on our own. 'Surely the rescue services must be making their way towards us as we speak?'

'No, because every single train on every line will be stalled like this. Even if half of the staff hadn't been laid off during the financial crisis, there's no way they could rescue every single tube passenger in London.'

And the more we discussed it, the clearer the scale of the problem became. If the power had gone down across the whole of Europe, if computers were crashing across the whole world, there was no limit to what else might be happening at this moment. Traffic lights would have stopped working, air traffic control would have ceased to function, miners would be trapped below ground, mariners would be cut off from land.

'It'll be like that New York blackout in the '70s. Everyone will either go out looting or go to bed and have it off.'

'Fortunately we can't do any looting in a tube train,' I said.

The other passengers looked at me uncertainly.

'Er, or have sex either,' I added hastily. 'I mean, neither of those really applies to this situation.'

The point was that, given the scale of the meltdown above ground, our situation could have actually been a lot worse. We were stationary in a London tube tunnel. At least we did not feel that our lives were in any imminent danger. That was to come with the next announcement from Jubilee Line information.

2

It seemed a cruel twist of fate that the last
view of England I might ever see was Neasden
Railway Depot. Generations of departing
soldiers had glanced back at the white cliffs
of Dover. I would have to make do with the
abiding image of rows of grubby tube trains
lined up in the drizzle across acres of weedy
train tracks. Neasden is also the location of the
only level crossing on the entire Underground
network. And *still* it struggles to attract the
tourists.

With what might be hours to kill waiting
in this tunnel, I stared up at the map of the

Underground line I knew so well. The Jubilee
is the only line to intersect with every other
line on the London Underground. It was very
late in the evolution of the network that it
finally developed a spine. Much of it had once
been part of the Metropolitan, the very first
line, which dates back a hundred and fifty
years to when steam trains ran underground,
and soot and smoke had filled the tunnels and
the passengers' lungs. And then in the 1970s it
morphed into the last Underground line to be
created: the 'Jubilee Line', so called because its
opening had missed the Queen's Silver Jubilee
by two whole years. I remembered the mild
controversy of it from my teens. Originally
named after a forgotten London river which
it roughly followed, the 'Fleet Line' had
seen new tunnels being dug between Baker
Street and Charing Cross. But then, without
consulting London Transport, the leader of the
Conservative-controlled GLC declared that the
Fleet Line would adopt this royalist moniker.
Hundreds of thousands of pounds' worth of

signage and maps were replaced, and no one dared object in case they appeared unpatriotic or anti-royal.

There had been further contrived outrage when a whole branch of the Bakerloo was cravenly surrendered to this upstart. Local transport historians and nomenclature pedants were never the most powerful lobbies in British politics, and everything from Baker Street to Stanmore was duly rebranded silver/grey instead of brown. This was the Jubilee Line's Louisiana Purchase, its quantum leap westward, more than doubling its dimensions and significance.

Commuters were indignant at this *fait accompli*: they reminded each other that this wasn't really the Jubilee Line, it had always been the Bakerloo Line. And they didn't like being told that actually, it hadn't. Until 1939 it had been a branch of the Metropolitan, but that year I suppose there were more significant changes on the world map to worry about.

Each station conjured up its own image for

me: a popular destination nearby, a personal memory or some inconsequential view that had lodged in my brain. But before this journey I had never seen how the Jubilee Line symbolized the history of modern capitalism, from 1930s Stanmore to twenty-first-century Stratford. That story, or rather differing interpretations of that story, would decide our way out of there. And, consequently, the matter of whether we lived or died.

'This is a Jubilee Line information update. Due to the ongoing power failure the Thames tunnel, currently undergoing essential strengthening work, is no longer safe. The hydraulic buttresses have ceased to function and sensors indicate the tunnel wall will not withstand the pressure at high tide. In order to avoid drowning, customers are advised to alight from the train and make their way on foot away from the direction of the tunnel. We apologize for any inconvenience this may have caused.'

Perhaps that huge rush of air that comes down tube tunnels is caused by the collective gasps of passengers reacting to London Transport's announcements. But on this occasion our astonishment and incredulity was more than justified. On hearing this fateful news, I was ready to panic and scream and rush towards the adjoining doors, probably knocking an elderly lady out of the way as I did so. But even in nightmares, the pressure for social conformity is a powerful one, and so when everyone else in the carriage just shook their heads in amused disbelief, and said how ridiculous this was, I secretly felt a little foolish for having so misjudged the appropriate response.

There was more than one tunnel under the Thames! How they laughed at this typical corporate cock-up. Did you ever hear anything so ridiculous? Telling us to walk away from the tunnel when we were currently in between two river crossings!

'That is classic!' chuckled one man.

'Priceless!' laughed another.

No other tube line crosses the river more

than once on a single journey. But the Jubilee
Line passes under the Thames four times
in total, and we were currently somewhere
between Waterloo and Canada Water. On any
other line the wording of that announcement
would be fine, but they had told us to move
'away from the direction of the tunnel' without
saying which one was about to collapse! I tried
my best to laugh along with everyone else at
London Transport's incompetence, at their
failure to tell us which direction was likely safety
and which was almost certain death.

In fact it was actually quite annoying to be
told that we might all be going to die by a voice
that sounded like the supermarket automaton
informing you of Unexpected Item in Bagging
Area. I was particularly struck by the use of the
word 'alight'. You don't 'alight' from a burning
tank, you jump for your life: Kate Winslet didn't
'alight' from the sinking *Titanic*, she 'leapt', she
'plummeted' into the freezing Atlantic. The
robot voice might have at least sounded a little
bit panicky; a raised voice or a swear-word

would not have gone amiss. Something like: '*This is Jubilee Line information. Fuckin' 'ell, there is some serious shit happening further up the tunnel, guys, and you wanna get the hell out of there fucking pronto!*'

Perhaps the monotonous message had done its job, because among my fellow passengers there were no screams or stampedes, there was no chaotic burst of activity.

'We should get the hell out of here!' I said.

'But in which direction?'

'Does it really matter which way we go?' I ventured. 'It must be less than half a mile to the nearest station in either direction. We could do that in ten minutes and then we are up the stairs to safety.'

'You're forgetting something . . .' said the man in the Real Ale T-shirt, who I had learned was called Jim. 'The Jubilee Line has barriers along the edge of the platforms. The electric doors will be closed against us. We might have to walk miles. In the dark.'

This information had taken the jeopardy to a new level. Now I was beginning to panic.

'If the barriers have all been closed,' said Jim, 'then the nearest open-air station is the Metropolitan platform at Baker Street.'

There was a moment of silence while we took in the gravity of our predicament. Or at least, I presumed that's what my fellow passengers must be doing.

'Baker Street. Oh, I like that one,' said the man in the England shirt.

'What?'

'Baker Street. You know, the song? I like that one.'

'Could we *please* concentrate on the matter at hand?' I pleaded.

'Did you know Bob Holness played the sax solo on that track?' said Jim.

'Who?'

'Bob Holness – the bloke who used to present *Blockbusters*. He was a mate of Gerry Rafferty and he played the famous saxophone riff.' And then he hummed the tune very badly, and the stupid couple smiled in recognition and started to hum along.

'Hello! Er, I think we have more urgent things to discuss right now,' I said, and then heard myself adding, 'but as a matter of fact, he didn't.'

'He did. It's a well-known fact.'

'It's not; it's an urban myth. But what's more important is that we have to decide which way we're going to go in order to save our lives. Not whether or not some deceased TV celebrity made a cameo appearance on a 1970s chart-topper. Although, for the record, he didn't.'

'I'm sure he did.'

'He didn't.'

'He did.'

'All right, let's say he did then!' I conceded. 'It doesn't matter! Can we please decide what we are going to do about getting out of this death trap?'

My stark description seemed to ratchet up the tension: people looked forlornly at one another until the silence was broken by Jim.

'It wasn't a chart-topper.'

'What?'

'You called "Baker Street" a chart-topper. It only got to number three.'

'Really?' said the England shirt. 'Wow – you've got a good memory.'

'I do a lot of pub quizzes.'

'Oh, right. What was number one then?'

'I don't mean to be rude,' I cut in, 'but at this very moment, millions of tonnes of freezing cold river water may be thundering down the tunnel towards us, about to fill up this carriage and drown us all. I would say remembering the song that kept "Baker Street" off the number one spot is NOT OUR TOP PRIORITY.'

There was a silence.

'Can't remember. Abba maybe?'

I looked at the tube map again, hoping for some sort of instant inspiration about what we should do. Staring at the geometric blue bar that represented the River Thames, I suddenly realized that this iconic diagram had been lying to me all this time. It had all the tube lines going *over* the river, not under. I'd never noticed that before. Was this a deliberate lie to reassure commuters? Were they worried that otherwise we might start wondering, 'Hang on, how the hell do they keep out all those billions of tonnes of water directly above us?'

'Does anyone know anything about engineering or which tunnel would be the most likely one to cave in or whatever?' I said to the whole carriage.

Now I felt grateful to have Jim on board: his quiz-trained brain was not just limited to useless trivia. 'There is "Essential Tunnel Strengthening" going on under the river between Waterloo and Westminster,' he said. 'But also under the Thames between Canada Water and Canary Wharf.'

'How do you know all this?'

'I stop and read the London Transport signs about all the planned engineering works. Doesn't everyone?'

This prompted the most unified response from the various characters on this carriage that I ever heard. 'No!' we all said at once.

'So which is the one likely to be giving way?'

I asked him hopefully. 'Which one should we start running away from?'

'Hmmm . . . Impossible to say . . .' he mused, perhaps enjoying the fact that his in-depth knowledge of engineering works on the London Underground had made him the centre of attention for possibly the only occasion in his life.

'It's ridiculous!' said the man in the England shirt. 'I don't know why they can't just sort it all out.' He had stood up, only to discover he couldn't look out the window. On the back of his football shirt was the name 'Terry', although the shirt itself was possibly a cheap imitation from the market. I was pretty sure the England badge didn't have *four* lions.

'I mean how hard can it be?' agreed his cross wife. 'They need to get in there and sort it all out, that's what they need to do. Sort it all out.'

If only we had had some means of communicating this genius insight to the engineers back at the LT control centre. The couple continued to talk nonsense very loudly, almost goading the rest of us into correcting their factual inaccuracies and false assumptions.

'If we are, like, rescued, will the fireman or whatever remember to swipe our Oyster cards as they carry us past the barriers?'

'Why would they be carrying us?' said Jim.

'They have to, don't they? Over their shoulder. It's part of Health and Safety.'

'We could lean down and swipe our own cards as they carry us past.'

'They'd better not charge us for this!' said his wife. 'I want a refund for this journey. I'm getting my money back when we get out of here.'

'Yeah,' said her husband, 'except we didn't exactly pay when we got on. We jumped the barriers like we always do.'

'Is London always like this?' said a nervy Yorkshireman in an anorak. 'We've never been before – and everyone back home was like, "Ooh what d'yer want to go to London for? It's right dangerous, London is, you'll be mugged or stabbed or summat, you don't want to go to London."'

'No, it's not always like this,' said Jim. 'This is an extremely unusual situation.'

'We won't be coming back to London, will we, dear? Not after all this fuss . . .'

'Look, sorry, but we are in really serious trouble here!' I blurted. 'If the tide is rising like they said, we could just be sitting here waiting to die and yet we're doing nothing, like those frogs in the pan of water.'

This analogy was greeted with a blank stare and so I was forced to explain the cliché that if frogs are placed in boiling water they jump straight out. But if they are placed in a pan of cold water that is gradually brought to the boil, they will remain there and die. The cross woman was horrified at this information.

'Why would you put a frog in a pan of boiling water?' she said.

'I wouldn't – I'm just making a point.'

'I mean how did you find that out? Did you boil a frog just for the hell of it?'

'No, of course I didn't boil a frog. It's just one

of those things they say, isn't it? Some scientists must have done an experiment.'

'Oh, and you are happy to take their word for it? "I torture frogs so everyone listen to me!" I can't believe you actually endorse live frog-boiling.'

Terry nodded in agreement. 'Disgusting!'

'I don't endorse live frog-boiling. This is ridiculous. I was just making the point that we are sitting here, and the danger is increasing, and we should be jumping out, not letting the temperature gradually rise.'

'Does it work with other amphibians?' said the Yorkshireman.

'What?'

'Like newts, for example?'

'But they can't really jump like a frog,' chipped in someone else.

'I think we should drop the whole analogy. I wish I'd never brought it up.'

'Please?' said the Turkish woman. 'Stratford?'

'We have to make a decision!' I said,

standing up. 'One of the tunnels is going to collapse. Our lives depend on escaping in the opposite direction. This guy here says there are engineering works on the river tunnels at Waterloo *and* at Canary Wharf. So there must be some historical engineering or geological factors we could take into account. Let's at least decide which direction gives us the best chance.'

'It's actually very interesting,' said Jim, 'because there are different agencies involved in the two works. Lambeth Council are working in partnership with London Transport on the Waterloo site. Whereas the Canary Wharf tunnel refurbishment is fully contracted out to private corporations, despite objections about them being non-unionized and using workfare trainees.'

'So there's the choice we have to make,' said a beautiful thirty-something blonde woman in a business suit. 'Who would you trust not to cock up an important building job? Some lefty Labour local authority working with an unwieldy nationalized institution? Or an efficient and innovative private company using the latest methods, unbound by red tape and the demands of the unions?'

'Definitely!' said Terry. 'Well then, let's get off the train and start walking down the tunnel towards Docklands.'

It was then that the elderly academic spoke up. 'Not necessarily,' he said in a gentle but assured voice. 'Pressure to produce dividends for shareholders can lead to corners being cut and safety precautions being skipped. If we have to make a choice, I would urge us to head away from the privately maintained tunnel.'

'Definitely!' said Terry. 'I agree with him. We should go the other way then, towards Westminster.'

And so it was that the underground version of a balloon debate began. The jury was a dozen or so typical tube passengers, including a Polish builder called Marek, a shy Asian student, the disappointed couple on their first trip to London from Yorkshire and this unassuming academic called Anthony something – I felt I should have recognized his name when he told me.

Over the next hour or so we had to decide which tunnel, in our opinion, was most likely to be shoddy and dangerous and more likely to collapse. The private one or the public one? The capitalist one or the socialist one? The Tory one or the Labour one? It was a debating society with a difference. Our lives depended upon making the right choice.

'*This is Jubilee Line information. We apologize for failing to specify which tunnel customers should move away from when abandoning the train. This was due to an oversight in our control room, and we are very sorry for not being clearer.*'

3

I had always proudly considered myself to
be on the left of the political spectrum. OK,
I didn't go on demonstrations any more, but if
there was a good cause mentioned on Facebook,
I always clicked on 'Like'. I did the sudoku in
the *Guardian*, deciding that the sudokus in the
Murdoch papers were unprincipled and sleazy.
I was clear that Nelson Mandela was a good
person, whereas Nick Griffin was bad, definitely.
Bad *and* fat.

But making political choices never particularly
inconvenienced me; my life carried along the
same comfortable privileged course whichever

progressive candidate I voted for. I gave small amounts to charity when I knew I could afford everything else I wanted. I didn't have a painful medical condition that would have to be endured for months if I didn't pay for a private operation. I didn't have children so didn't have to choose between a state or private school. My vague socialism was an easy fashion choice that made me look urban and tolerant and, I hoped, perhaps vaguely intellectual. I agreed with more government spending on almost everything; I disagreed with more taxes for almost everybody. That's the wonder of Western democracy: very limited power but zero responsibility.

But suddenly my life depended on my *deep* political convictions. At this moment my real beliefs had major consequences for *me*. Nothing focuses the mind like the prospect of immediate drowning in some dark tunnel deep underground: now I would have to be very, very sure of what I actually believed. Was I really certain that I thought privatization was a bad thing? Had I just lazily accepted the easy, worthy position on public provision being a positive notion – or was I actually prepared to stake my life upon the routine opinions I nodded along with when comedians got a round of applause on *Question Time*.

'So, we have to make a choice,' reiterated Anthony, the man I had cast as some sort of university professor. 'Walk through the tunnels towards Westminster if we think the council and nationalized corporation will be safest. Or walk towards free market Docklands and Canary Wharf if we think that the best job will have been done by the private sector.'

'But how long have we got?'

'High tide in the Port of London is at 12.57 hours,' said Jim.

'How on earth do you know what time high tide is in London?' I asked him.

'I read all the tidal timetables printed in the newspaper. Doesn't everyone?'

'Well then,' said Anthony. 'We have no more than an hour to debate what we are to do. Whether we go east or west, choose left or right, and whether we do it together or each choose to go our own way.'

There was an anxious glance from seat to seat: a search for a leader or a suggestion. Terry got out a cigarette and went to light it.

'Excuse me!' said the smart-looking blonde lady. 'You can't smoke on the London Underground!'

'Sod that, we might all be dead soon, luv. There's no point in worrying about lung cancer now, is there? I need a ciggie and this might be the last one I ever smoke.'

'In which case,' said Jim, 'can I have one too?'

A match was struck.

'Fuck off! At seven quid a packet?'

'Well,' said the blonde, 'I still don't think that society collapsing and us all being fatally trapped in a tunnel gives you the right to be so rude.'

Smoke seemed to fill the carriage immediately.

'That goes to the very heart of our debate, doesn't it?' suggested Anthony. 'Smoking in the presence of others is at the crux of the debate about individual freedom versus the rights of the wider community. Amazingly the Metropolitan Railway wished to ban smoking on the Underground back at the very beginning when the first section opened.'

He had stood and was pointing at the tube map to illustrate his point.

'It took an amendment to an Act of Parliament to force the Underground to permit smoking for its first 120 years. Victorian legislators thought a ban would be an infringement of traditional liberties.'

'What's that got to do with the safest way out of here?'

'Because it is the same argument. Is *what I want as a free individual* the same thing as *what is best for society as a whole*? Adam Smith and the Victorian capitalists believed so. But now all mainstream political parties seem to have agreed that we do not have the right to harm each other's well-being with cigarettes or leaded petrol or lax health and safety procedures. But

if our *economic* activity harms others, if we take
huge risks with other people's pension funds
or buy out their company and make them
redundant, that is somehow acceptable. That,'
he declared conclusively, 'is why the Docklands
tunnel will burst first – because there is no
equivalent of the smoking ban in modern
capitalism.'

There was a moment's silence.

'All right, mate,' said Terry, opening his
packet of cigarettes. 'You can have one.'

Then the smart blonde lady quietly said, 'No,
you're wrong.'

'Well, luv, if he's wrong, all that flood-water
will put our fags out anyway.' But only he and
his wife laughed.

'I have something of an interest in politics
myself, as it happens. And the idea that our
society imposes no restrictions on economic
activity is clearly fallacious . . .'

'Sounds disgusting,' smirked Terry.

'Fallacious – deceptive. Capitalism may not
be perfect, but it is the reason we are not still

living in bucolic squalor, dying at thirty-five from the plague. The gentleman indicates the tube map. But look at the map of the Jubilee Line: this is the story of progress, of innovation, of entrepreneurial capitalism that made the modern world and so much that we previously took for granted.'

I found myself nodding, but then realized that I had responded far too early: she hadn't actually explained why yet. This Conservative supporter was clearly not from the same tribe as myself and we should have had very little in common. But I listened to her attentively and sympathetically, smiling and agreeing for one very valid reason. The advocate for capitalism was very beautiful. I suppose it was sort of appropriate that the representative of the consumer society, the person on the side of big business and advertising corporations, should be shiny and sexy and enticing and completely out of the reach of any of us.

I noticed most of the men in the carriage perking up as Caroline continued. (Each of the men had taken the first opportunity to introduce themselves to her.) Here we were trying to decide what was best for our very chances of living or dying, and still it seemed it was not possible to weigh the evidence and arguments objectively. The attractiveness or otherwise of the proponents was a factor, even now.

'The Jubilee Line was opened in the very week that Margaret Thatcher became Prime Minister,' she began. 'May 1979. Britain was a country crippled by strikes and intransigent unions, where the inefficiency of the public sector was meekly accepted with a resigned shrug. See there where this line heads out to Docklands? That was her government's decision; the original route for the Jubilee Line extension was headed towards dying industries and decreasing populations. But she didn't just change the route of this tube line; she changed the entire direction of economic activity in Britain. Over a million fewer people worked in the public sector by the time she left office.

Britain's economy boomed in the 1980s, services improved in the liberated free market, and when Labour got back in, they knew not to re-nationalize the coal mines, the major utilities or indeed the railways. This train we are sitting in was travelling *away* from Westminster. That is the right direction to be going in – away from excessive government interference – towards the free market of her Docklands Enterprise Zone. You turn back if you want to; ignore everything that the last forty years has taught us. But none of you would choose a council flat over a private apartment; you wouldn't choose school dinners over a high-street restaurant, so why would you suddenly opt to trust your life to a botched local authority repair job?'

She sat down, leaving the carriage in speechless contemplation. Her certainty made me reassess what I thought I believed; perhaps everyone else was reflecting on the same thing. Either way, the silence gave Anthony his opportunity to respond. I wanted him to be right; I wanted him to persuade me.

'The tube map does tell you everything you need to know,' he began. 'A perfect example of the folly of abandoning everything to market forces. Different companies competing against each other with no central planning authority to ensure that local travellers were best served. A tube journey from Ruislip to West Ruislip for example would require you to change four times, using three different lines and passing twenty-two stations. Why? Because no single government or London authority compelled the competing entrepreneurs to put an interchange where the Central Line crossed the rival Metropolitan Line. The same thing happens where the red crosses the blue above Park Royal, not to mention that you can't get to Euston from the Circle Line. All over London, and indeed the whole of Britain, there are insane railway lines that don't work as a logical entity: small towns like Southend or Dartford or Windsor that have two competing railway stations, demonstrating what happens if you don't have the rules and planning that might have got in the way of a quick buck.'

Sitting there listening to this elderly intellectual in his slightly worn suit, I learned how the railway boom of the nineteenth century had actually set the template for modern industrial capitalism. The outlay required for the largest infrastructure project since the Romans had been too vast to be funded by a few rich dukes and factory owners; it demanded a relaxation of the strict rules regarding limited share issues and capital funding. It needed the sort of mass capitalist speculation that had been banned following the pre-industrial crash of the South Sea Bubble. Such is the cyclical pattern of financial safeguards, he explained. There is a major economic collapse such as 1929. Regulations are brought in to prevent it ever happening again. After a few decades, the money-makers complain about excessive restrictions, and precisely because they are rich and influential they get their way and are set free to take greater risks with other people's money all over again. And eventually there is another crash like 2008, which is precisely the reason that we were all stuck underground wondering if we would ever get out again.

He pointed to the map of the Jubilee Line once more. 'This route neatly illustrates the triumph of capital over communities during the last eighty years or so. The line starts at Stanmore, an unassuming terminus built with room for three or four commercial units serving local needs. A small barber's, a travel agent's and a minicab office called 'Jubilee Cars', if my memory serves me . . .'

'Maybe that's how the line got its name,' said Terry's wife, who then seemed mildly put out that this point was completely ignored by everyone else in the carriage.

'That was the full extent of the commercialization of the site when it was built back before the war. But as the Jubilee Line heads towards the capital, the potential for extracting profit from customers grows more avaricious at each stop. Through the traditional high streets of Willesden and the more salubrious St John's Wood, until it reaches

Bond Street, at the time of its construction an out-of-town shopping centre every bit as brash and bold as Bluewater or Lakeside, Thurrock. In fact Harry Selfridge lobbied hard to have this station named "Selfridge's", but the authorities resisted.'

I hadn't known that fact, but I could understand why they had. Once they conceded one department store the right to give its name to a station, then all sorts of other shops might have demanded free advertising in this way. '*Customer information, this is a Tesco Metro Line train via Primark. Customers wishing to travel via What She Wants should change at Mr One-Pound, formerly Woolworths.*'

Anthony continued to trace his finger along the map. 'The line whisks its way towards the greatest financial trading centre in the world, before finally ending up at Stratford East, the largest shopping centre in the whole of Europe. A journey that begins with just a trickle of small-scale commercial activity ends with a torrent of big money, where global brands have displaced local communities, the ultimate triumph of profit over people.'

The Polish man was concentrating hard, and Anthony noticed this and spoke more slowly.

'Perhaps some of you have heard that terrifying statistic that as you head east out of central London on the Jubilee Line, average life expectancy declines by one year for every underground stop that you pass. How can it be that commercial power grows ever more voracious as you travel down the line, and yet the power of people to control their own lives gets weaker at every station? Power is supposed to reside *here*, at Westminster, with the politicians we elect. But instead it resides *here*, in the City and Docklands, with the banks who own our homes, our companies and our pension funds. We thought we had "one man, one vote". But in reality it is "one dollar, one vote". The private repair is being done for profit. Only public work will make ordinary people's safety paramount whatever the cost. On that tube map, as in life, we should turn left.'

It was a powerful performance: I almost felt a compulsion to applaud. Now I felt certain that I agreed with him. The socialist said we should get out of the back of the train. The Conservative said we should escape via the front of the train. Part of me wished Tony Blair was there just to see him explain how there was in fact a 'Third Way'.

'Well, love – he's got you there, hasn't he?' said Terry, stubbing out his cigarette on the floor. 'You say power's in one place, he says it's somewhere else. I say there is no bloody power, which is why we are stuck here between London Bridge and Bermondsey!' And his wife laughed as required.

'It's in both,' said Caroline, taking her cue. 'Westminster does have real power. City Hall here at London Bridge has other powers. And of course the multinationals and banks in the financial district here have their own type of power. But any of them can use their influence for good or ill. My opponent talks about central planning as if government

always makes the right plans . . .' She pointed
to North Greenwich Station. 'But remember
the Millennium Dome? That's what happens
when government decides how to plan the
nation's entertainment rather than leave it to
the free market. Tony Blair was desperate to
get the Jubilee Line out to North Greenwich
in time for the grand opening and so the line
went massively over budget. The electrician
unions working on that line were dubbed 'the
Untouchables'. They could demand any pay
increase they fancied because strikes would
have meant missing the immovable deadline of
31 December 1999.'

I had completely forgotten how incredibly
cross we all were with Tony Blair about the
Dome. The unpopularity of this expensive
white elephant had been bad enough during
its construction. But then on the night that it
opened, they made perhaps an elementary error
in the world of PR and branding, which is to
give all the attendant journalists and opinion-
formers a really, really terrible time. When

Prince sang about partying like it was 1999, I don't think he imagined hundreds of well-connected North London media types queuing up for three hours at North Greenwich tube station, shouting at harassed security officers, 'Do you know who I bloody am?'

'The private sector would never have allowed the Dome to be such a mishmash of worthy causes and impenetrable zones,' continued the counsel for capitalism. 'There's no "Faith Zone" at Alton Towers because the attractions have been dictated by market forces rather than political pressure. And it turns out' – she allowed herself a smile – 'that Alton Towers' terrifying high-speed roller coaster is actually a safer journey than this mundane Underground train. Because unlike a state-sponsored transport system, one major accident at a theme park would be enough to finish them off for ever. That's why the privately repaired tunnel will be safest. Because the companies can't afford it not to be. The public sector won't be put out of business by their own mistakes.'

This debate had become utterly infuriating because I found myself agreeing with both of them. They were making it so difficult for me to take a short cut and jump to one side or the other. Why couldn't she have had a patronizing manner or a self-congratulatory laugh, which would have made it so much easier to decide who I wanted to identify with? Why couldn't he have been rambling and boring so that I wouldn't have found myself so interested in the complex points he was making? But no, Anthony had to be gentle and charming and quietly persuasive, and she insisted on being provocative and attractive and charismatic.

The debate went back and forth, and I learned how the building contractors had underpinned Big Ben to stop it falling over during the excavations at Westminster Station. I learned how the revised route of the Jubilee Line extension had left a ghost platform at Charing Cross. And I learned that St John's Wood was the only tube station not to contain a letter from the word 'mackerel'. Jim in ·

particular was a goldmine of useless facts
that did nothing to assist the discussion. He
recounted how one station on the line used to
be called 'West End' (hence West End Lane),
but the Victorians foresaw that this might cause
problems with coachloads of theatregoers
mistakenly turning up there to see Lloyd-
Webber musicals. So West End acquired the
new name 'West Hampstead'. I couldn't help
thinking that '*Not* Hampstead' might have been
more honest.

Anthony explained that the Jubilee Line
extension was the only tube line to be built
to satisfy the demands of a private developer
rather than the proven needs of Londoners.
Olympia and York, who built Canary Wharf,
had lobbied hard to have the extension built
to serve their major new development in
Docklands (although they hadn't wanted it
to bother with stopping in poor areas like
Bermondsey along the way). They promised
to pay a substantial part of the cost of the
new line, but, surprise, surprise, they ended

up paying less than 5 per cent as the taxpayer stepped in to pick up the difference yet again. He cited this as another example of how big business maximizes profits at the expense of the majority.

'But if so many people are always exploited as you say,' said Marek, 'why does everyone keep putting up with it?'

'Perhaps because our society has evolved coping mechanisms. So here at Southwark Cathedral, or the London Central Mosque at St John's Wood, or indeed the Swaminarayan Hindu Temple at Neasden, we are promised a better next life if we behave ourselves in this one. For others, a short-term fix of shopping anaesthetic can be prescribed here at Bond Street or the O2 Centre in Finchley Road. Or we divest our hopes into spheres where we have no actual control, putting disappointment in our own lives to one side if England wins here at Wembley Stadium, or West Ham United wins over here,' he said, pointing at the map.

'No way! West Ham? Scum!' said Terry,

finding a level at which he could contribute something.

I wish I could be as interesting and thought-provoking as Anthony and Caroline, I mused. Perhaps the time had come for me to make my own stimulating contribution to this debate? I looked at the map and saw Green Park. I remembered how the announcer had said, 'Exit here for Buckingham Palace,' which had surprised me as I couldn't really imagine the Queen ever getting the tube home, even less without some flunky to tell her which stop to get off at. How did the royal family fit into this debate, centred as it was on a tube line named after the Queen's anniversary and formally opened by Prince Charles: a totemic symbol for right-wing patriots and yet the epitome of centralized state funding?

'What about Kate Middleton?' I heard myself say.

'What about her?' the two of them replied in unison, which did not feel like a good sign.

'Well, you know, the Duchess of Cambridge

is basically inessential and yet the right would always maintain that the state should fund *her*.'

'I don't understand the point you are making,' said Caroline.

'Well, under your system, Kate really ought to make a profit. You know, people should have to pay for her visits . . .'

There was a puzzled pause before the cross lady said, 'Are you suggesting that we should make Kate a prostitute? Is that what you want? Turn our lovely Kate into a common whore?'

'No – I never said that!' I exclaimed.

'That's bang out of order that is. I'm all for private enterprise and all that, but I can't agree with the frog-boiler if he wants to force Kate Middleton into prostitution.'

'This is ridiculous!'

'Like William hasn't suffered already! It's not enough for you that he loses his poor mum to a murder plot. You want him humiliated as well.'

'You could charge quite a lot though,' pondered her husband unhelpfully.

'I don't even want to think about it.'

'American businessmen. Wealthy Arabs. They'd pay a fortune to give Kate Middleton one. I know I would if I had the dosh. This geezer might have actually come up with the solution to Britain's national debt.'

Then the tannoy crackled and there was another announcement.

'This is Jubilee Line information. Customers are advised that the Thames tunnel has now given way and river water is flooding the line. Please allow passengers off the train before boarding. Boarding. Mind the . . . Customers. This train is for. This train is for. Gap. Gap. Change here for mainline . . . Mind the . . . Please remember to take all your belongings with you.'

And then the lights went out.

4

There were a couple of screams and then
someone uttered a reassuring, 'It's OK! It's all
right . . .' into the darkness. 'I've got a torch on
my iPhone! Hang on . . .'

'Hurry up! Put it on!'

'Yeah and I've got a torch on my Nokia.'
A brief pause while phones were searched for.
'Actually they reckon it lasts longer than the
iPhone one.'

'Yeah, but the Nokia doesn't have all the
other apps.'

'Can we just get some light in here,' I suggested,
'instead of arguing about who has got the best

new phone?' It was ridiculous that this still seemed to matter. The fact that I had a really rubbish mobile phone with no light or camera was completely beside the point.

A bright light was shone directly at me, which despite making me squint failed to light up the carriage very much.

'There! See, there's another reason I vote Tory,' said Terry, who hadn't actually told us this until now. 'You'd never get government-issue iPhones.'

'Thank you for applying to iGov for the "Hot Babes in Bikinis" app,' chuckled Caroline, taking up the theme. 'Your application is currently being processed and will be downloaded to your device in six to eight weeks.'

'Exactly!' said Anthony. 'Because people don't actually *need* "Hot Babes in Bikinis". They need housing and hospitals and schools, and a public transport system that doesn't seize up because the bankers have crippled the economy. So by all means allow the free market to supply the iPhone applications, and the latest electronic gadgets, and a skinny Frappuccino with vanilla swirl or whatever. But if we all *depend* on something, if everyone in society *must have it*, then the state is the only agency with the power and authority to ensure that there will be a fire station in your town but no carcinogenic additives in your children's food.'

'Look, it seems to me that we are never going to agree,' I said. 'Is there not some sort of unarguable test, some ultimate decider that can resolve this debate once and for all?'

Then, in my dream, the lights flickered back on to reveal that both Noam Chomsky and Roger Scruton just happened to be on the train with us. Until then I had barely registered the two quiet old men sitting separately down the end of the carriage. But just when we needed this debate promptly settled, when we were struggling to come to any conclusion on the merits or otherwise of our Western political and economic system, we were able to call upon two of its most prominent philosophical thinkers as witnesses.

'This collapse is inevitable,' declared Chomsky

without even being asked to commence his analysis, 'because the US-dominated world economy has seen state capitalism create a new slave trade of the nominally waged.'

'Oh, shut it, Chomsky, you four-eyed pseud,' snapped Roger Scruton, lowering his copy of *National Trust News*.

'Oh no, not fucking Scruton!' groaned the American. 'Just my luck to be trapped on a tube train with a right-wing rural relic like you! The whole reason we are stuck here is because of you and all your corporate fascist fellow-travellers in the industrial military complex.'

'I think not, O Colonial Schoolteacher. It is the very lack of real aesthetic freedom that has dragged our political and economic system to its knees. Your neo-liberal apologists have bound the beautiful beast with a thousand miles of red tape.'

Almost immediately the insults were flying back and forth with most onlookers struggling to understand much of what was being said. But the core philosophical point under examination shifted subtly, from the neo-liberal settlement and its fallout, to whether or not Chomsky was a 'commie shithead'.

'Oh yeah?' said Chomsky aggressively, standing nose to nose with the Academic of Aesthetics.

'Yeah!' Scruton was not going to blink first.

'You philosopher-terrorists need to be taught a lesson from the people who actually keep spiritual order and liberty in this world.'

'Oh yeah? You and *whose* army?'

'Well, NATO's . . .'

I tried to calm things down. 'Look, come on, guys. Just trading insults isn't going to resolve anything . . .'

'Stay out of this, liberal quisling!'

'Yeah, shut it, gaylord!'

Their hostility to my attempted intervention was the only thing on which they seemed to agree. I found it particularly bizarre that Roger Scruton had just unleashed a homophobic playground insult in my direction.

'Fight! Fight! Fight!' chanted Terry and his cross wife.

We'd been getting nowhere debating the philosophical merits of traditionalist capitalism or anarcho-syndicalism, and so instead Noam Chomsky and Roger Scruton were going to fight it out. For a split second I thought Scruton had backed down, because he turned away, his expression suggesting he couldn't be bothered with such a political pygmy as the author of *Profit over People: Neoliberalism and Global Order*. But this deft move was a feint to catch the American off his guard, and in a split second Scruton turned and planted a fierce left hook into the mouth of his philosophical nemesis.

There was a gasp at the sight of the Emeritus Academic of Linguistics at the Massachusetts Institute of Technology with blood running between his teeth, and for a moment it appeared that the fight might be over before it had even begun. But suddenly, with a loud roar, Chomsky charged at Scruton and sent him staggering back against the carriage doors, pummelling his kidneys, and then slamming his knee up into the testicles of the author of *Culture Counts: Faith and Feeling in a World Besieged.*

Scruton, now red-faced and seemingly incandescent with fury, hit back, landing a punch that caught Chomsky in the eye, breaking the glasses that the linguistic academic really should have removed before all this had started. There was a split second when they both caught their breath, but it was clear their philosophical differences were too great to leave things there and the two of them traded wild, poorly aimed punches that hit ears or necks or shoulder blades.

When the fight had looked imminent I had wondered whether Scruton had ever studied any martial arts. Perhaps his life-long quest for spiritual meaning and his love of tradition and culture might have drawn him to Japanese kendo or karate? But the only cultural combat style in his armoury was the Glasgow kiss, a full-blown head-butt that he landed right on Chomsky's nose, sending an audible crack across the carriage and pouring blood over both of them. The screams and shouts gradually gave way as the fight now entered the clumsy, grappling stage, both of them writhing around the carriage floor among the discarded newspapers and the blackened deposits of gum. The American had Scruton in a headlock, but the founder and editor of the *Salisbury Review* was not done yet, and he bit Chomsky as hard as he could on the forearm, bringing a surprisingly high-pitched scream from the American cognitive scientist.

'You fight like a fucking girl, Scruton!' snarled Chomsky.

'There can be no beauty in violence, except in nature,' declared Scruton, who then burst into tears. The combatants were clearly exhausted and now just lay there panting and whimpering, seeming to have reached a bruised and bloodied stalemate that failed to resolve the key moral, philosophical and political questions of our age.

I took a moment to register that the fight had petered out before I turned to Anthony and asked him whether war between ideologies was inevitable. Was this violence 'inherent in the system', as claimed by Karl Marx and that peasant in the Monty Python film?

'No, of course it isn't,' interjected Caroline.

'I think it probably is,' he insisted.

'What clichéd Marxist nonsense!'

'It IS NOT nonsense –'

'All right,' I interjected. 'Don't you two have a punch-up as well.'

The insane thing was that even though these two old men had thoroughly kicked the shit out of one another, the spilling of blood hadn't actually resolved anything. All we had learnt was that Scruton couldn't 'have' Chomsky, who thought that Scruton 'fought like a girl', which frankly was a disappointingly sexist comment for one of the world's leading left-wing intellectuals.

What the fight did precipitate was some movement. The battered Chomsky declared that he could not bear to remain in the carriage a moment longer and unilaterally headed back down towards the rear of the train, slamming the connecting door behind him and muttering grumpily about British public transport.

As the two of them made their respective escapes, I squinted through the scratch-frosted window to the adjoining carriages. None of us had even considered involving passengers from the rest of the train in this debate; we existed only in our own political bubble. Like sovereign states each fighting their private elections to try and find a response to global economic or environmental forces, it wasn't so much what we said that was the problem, but the fact that we were saying it only to each other. Would the global crisis above ground precipitate the creation of a world government? Would the good people of Surrey West be prepared to vote according to the desperate needs of sub-Saharan Africa, to think about the deforestation of the Amazon basin or the oppression of billions of sweatshop workers and indentured campesinos? Maybe, but then they'd go and vote UKIP second preference.

Sometimes you saw people down by the

market selling newspapers calling for 'World Revolution', but that had always struck me as a logistical nightmare. Just setting the date would involve co-ordinating so many diaries. But at least they were thinking on the right scale; for the rest of us, it seemed that no matter how much we were buffeted by world economic and environmental events, our politics remained pathetically parochial.

But then you had to get everyone else interested. As I watched Noam Chomsky disappearing down through the adjoining carriage I saw him try to engage with a few passengers. They glanced up from their magazines and Kindles to see a battered, dusty old man with dishevelled hair and a bloody face shouting something at them about capitalism and their imminent death unless they followed him. And every single one of them quickly reverted to concentrating extra hard on the apparently gripping content of whatever they were reading. Clearly their fear that they might all be about to die in a horrific underground flood was not as great as their terror that the nutter on the tube was talking directly to them.

Although the two philosophers had gone off in opposite directions, it felt encouraging that a couple of people had at least made a decision. Jubilee Line information had helpfully told us that river water was now flushing through these empty pipes from one direction or the other and we could not remain where we were. The lights flickered a couple of times, to remind us that at any moment we might be cast into permanent darkness.

'OK, I'm getting out of here!' announced Caroline. 'Who is coming this way?'

'Which way please Stratford?' said the Turkish tourist.

'Stratford is that way,' I confirmed, pointing to where Caroline was already standing and holding the connecting door open. The lady stood up to go with Caroline, and for no other reason the cause of capitalism had already gathered a little momentum.

'I am going that way also,' said Marek.

'In Poland, socialism was very bad. England and America is better.'

'That's the point, isn't it?' said Jim. 'Socialism lost when the Berlin Wall came down.'

'Although it was a very well-made wall,' I pointed out. 'I mean, if you look at the newsreels, it takes them bloody ages to take the smallest chip out of it.'

'Oh no, you're right. You've got me all conflicted again now . . .'

'Yes, but which way did people rush when the wall came down?' said Caroline. 'Towards capitalism or away from it?'

'She's right,' said the cross woman. 'Come on, we're going with her.'

'Don't bloody tell me what to do!' Terry protested. 'Now follow me, we're going with her.'

The quiet Asian student also got up and moved towards the front of the train, followed by the couple down from Yorkshire. Soon Anthony was all alone, waiting to see if his only remaining ally would accompany him in the other direction.

'Well, I've always considered myself to be on the left,' I heard myself mumble. 'But I just don't know any more. It seems to me that some things are probably done best by individuals and private companies, and other things should be entrusted to the state or local authorities or whatever . . .'

My eye caught an advertisement done in the style of the tube map. The first station was called 'Tickly Cough'. The next stations were 'Runny Nose' and 'Blocked Sinuses'. And the slogan of the flu remedy advert was 'Stuck on the Influenza Line?' It really was a rubbish advert, unoriginal and laboured; it reminded me that low standards are certainly not the exclusive preserve of one sector or the other. Next to it was one of the 'Poems on the Underground' – twelve perfectly crafted lines that I had read and reread at the beginning of this journey. How fantastic that London Underground placed beautiful poetry alongside the advertisements, I thought. How utterly civilized and progressive to present a snippet of literature simply for the enjoyment of passengers, something that wasn't sponsored by a private corporation or trying to persuade us of anything. Would the private sector ever do anything as noble and altruistic as that?

I felt myself gravitate towards Anthony. 'Like I say, I have always thought of myself as being sort of on the left, so my gut is saying I should follow him.'

The old man was ready to set off with his one comrade, eager to get going. But I felt unnerved to be in the company of so many people who didn't share my politics. I had always been confident that my opinions on society, religion, life and everything else were indisputable because they had been continuously reinforced by a careful selection of friends who completely agreed with me. Or had it been the other way round? Were my opinions just reflections of the type of people I liked to mix with? I favoured a certain type of music, I had a particular taste in films; the liberal politics lazily fitted in with all of that.

And in that moment of maximum pressure

a terrible thought struck me. Had I only ever been on the left because I thought it was cool? Were my politics a posture, a fashion accessory? Clearly Che Guevara and John Lennon were always going to be hipper pin-ups than Jim Davidson and Carol Vorderman, but now that I was in my forties, did I just continue to espouse left-wing views because I thought it made me 'alternative'? Being against the system was a comfortable place to be. A luxury position that only this particular system tolerated.

The image of the crowds rushing through the gap in the Berlin Wall was stuck in my mind. Would Anthony and I have been trying to push our way past the throng as we battled our way into East Germany?

'So, time to go . . .' I mumbled. I felt myself avoiding Anthony's eye. That was when I realized I'd made a decision. 'Actually, Anthony, I'll probably carry on voting left. You know, if we ever get out of here . . . But in this particular instance . . . I think I'm going to try turning . . . right?'

My final words were barely a whisper. But I saw a triumphant smile flicker across Caroline's face, and at some deep subconscious level I worried that my decision was actually affected by the fact that I fancied her.

'That's OK,' said Anthony, taking only three syllables to make it clear that it wasn't. 'Good luck.'

'Good luck to you . . .'

And so we left him just standing there alone with his political faith, watching us leave him as we filed away through the connecting door towards the front of the train. I caught his reflection in the glass and it occurred to me that he might be the only survivor or the only victim from our carriage.

We moved quickly towards the front of the train, past the iPod-hypnotized zombies just waiting there in the other carriages, failing even to react to pleas to follow us. There was no sign of a driver or guard, and entrance to the driver's cab was quickly secured with an emergency handle. All of this happened way ahead of me: I was not a leader in the trek towards freedom, I was just a fellow traveller. Or perhaps now a bona fide 'customer'?

'*This is Jubilee Line information. Beggars may be operating on this train, please do not encourage them.*'

It didn't really seem like quite the right moment. Now we were squeezing out of the side of the cab and down on to solid ground. For one ridiculous moment I tried to stop my clothes brushing against the filthy tunnel wall, still not acknowledging the seriousness of this situation.

'No sign of any water yet,' someone said. I had always imagined any flood when it came would be a torrent, a dramatic and sudden tidal wave; it hadn't occurred to me that it might rise slowly from a puddle around our shoes.

A couple of phone torches were lighting my step down, and I could make out other glowing oblongs showing the way along the tunnel. Then, just as I was about to walk away from the train, I heard a familiar voice behind me.

'Hang on . . .' said Anthony.

To my shame, I felt disappointed to see him. We walked a few steps behind the rest of the party as they trudged eastwards amid questions about the live rail and instructions to stick together. Finally I found the courage to speak my mind.

'You argued so passionately that we should all go in the other direction, and now you are just opting for the private option like the rest of us?' My tone was more accusatory than I had intended. I had obviously decided that it was all right for me to go against what I'd previously believed, but I wanted him at least to remain true to his convictions even if it meant he had to die for them.

'I still believe in all those things I said back there,' said Anthony. 'But I trust in the principle of democracy even more fiercely. If everyone else in this carriage believes that I was wrong, then, well, I probably am.'

And he strode purposefully towards the pitch darkness ahead of us. 'Now this next section has a fascinating history . . .'

5

I didn't mind the trudge through the tunnel:
I knew what I had to do. This darkness
was preferable to the mental groping and
floundering I'd endured in the debate on
the carriage. We marched in single file and
I followed the glowing phones bobbing in the
darkness, still nervous of tripping on to the live
rails that Jim had assured us would be harmless.

'But how can you tell that the rail isn't live?'

'Well, it's very technical and complicated. But
if it was live, our train would have been moving
forward at twenty miles an hour and all the
lights would be on.'

Hundreds of thousands of people passed through these tunnels every week, but they all did so within the protective shell of a tube train. Now we were stripped of all armour, walking not riding, seeing close up what a deeply inhospitable place the Underground tunnels really were. Dirty, dangerous and dark; they even *smelt* grey.

Our unspoken hope was that we would emerge from the tunnel at the next station to find that the platform doors had been opened, or that there would be some sort of access hatch or emergency gate at the end of the station. But, of course, the one area where we have seen consistent lapses from the Health and Safety Executive has been an abject failure to implement appropriate safeguards in people's nightmares. Psychiatric patients never tell their counsellors, 'I dreamt I was falling and falling, but fortunately the council had installed a safety net and anyway I was wearing protective headgear.'

So of course the platform at Bermondsey

was closed off to us. There were no ventilation shafts or access tunnels. We could only gaze at this phantom station through a thick glass screen. Improvised torches could just make out the shapes of the smiling faces in the posters on the walls: exotic holidays in sunny, wide open spaces, as if mocking our desperate situation. Those of us at the back of the line sat on a rail and waited while half-hearted attempts were made to prise open the doors or smash the glass.

'So you came with us because you believe being a democrat is more important than being a socialist or a capitalist?' This is what now passed for casual chit-chat between myself and the old man seated beside me. 'You value the wisdom of the crowd above your own?'

'Well, any political system will bring disaster if dissent ends up being crushed and bad leaders cannot be removed.'

'So isn't the fact that we live in a democracy the end of the argument? The choice has been made.'

'It would be if our democracy was genuinely democratic. We talked about the various centres of power along the Jubilee Line: the political authority of Westminster, the economic muscle of the banks in Canary Wharf. But there is of course another major pillar supporting the current system: the power of the media.'

He tapped the rail on which we were sitting. 'This "Fleet Line" was supposed to go via Fleet Street, but both the newspapers and tube ended up moving east into the derelict docks as the opinion-formers followed the money. A real democracy must have a genuinely free press, yet here we are at Bermondsey, scene of one of the most infamous media stitch-ups of our lifetime. In 1983, at the point when the modern Labour Party had its most socialist agenda, a national tabloid hate campaign was waged against an openly gay left-wing candidate. And a secretly bisexual Liberal was elected in his place. Of course the *Sun* and the *Daily Mail* knew that both men were not straight, but told malicious lies about one and colluded in keeping secrets about the other. The result was one of the greatest by-election swings in British electoral history.'

I had only a vague memory of this episode, and it was hard to connect this dark tunnel with a forgotten political battle fought in the streets above us. 'But people were still basically free to vote for who they wanted in Bermondsey?' I suggested.

'Is that genuine freedom, though? If you are being lied to and don't know it? Isn't the ignorance and prejudice that is cultivated within our system its own form of imprisonment? Was it Goethe who said, "None are more hopelessly enslaved than those who falsely believe themselves to be free"?'

'Oh yeah. Goethe. Definitely.'

As we had anticipated, it had not been possible to get through the platform barriers at Bermondsey: we would just have to keep walking. I ran a forlorn hand along the glass screen for as long as it lasted but soon we were back in the inhospitable claustrophobia of the tunnel. This was the newest section on the entire Underground network, but tube tunnels do not stay clean and fresh for very long. Tube mice darted away, surprised to have their private quarters invaded like this. You could smell the oily soot that lined the walls and soaked into the fluff that accumulated around rivets and under rails.

Apparently the night workers who walk these lines clearing the litter from the tracks say you get a better quality of fluff in richer parts of London. At impoverished parts of the line like Canning Town or West Ham it is all viscose and nylon; in St John's Wood, it's more of a lambswool-cashmere mix. And yet there is still something classless about the London Underground: there is no first-class carriage or buffet car; everyone is crammed in together and suffers the shunts and smells and signal failures together.

I overheard a conversation just ahead of us.

'There's a little arrow on these cables pointing ahead to Canada.'

'I think they mean Canada *Water*? Because

if we were close to Canada *the country* we'd
be really fucking lost.'

When it came, Canada Water Station
was a space so magnificent in its scale and
architecture that you'd imagine it must be the
secret underground missile silo of a James Bond
villain rather than anything as mundane as a
tube station. The traditional broken chocolate
machine would have looked completely out of
place here. A solitary busker would get lost: you
would need a full gospel choir or the London
Symphony Orchestra. I'm sure they could
have worked out their own arrangement of
'Wonderwall'. There was no denying that the
youngest line on the London Underground had
set a new standard of scale and grandeur for
the stations they cared about. Jim commented
that you could actually fit one of the Canary
Wharf towers into Canary Wharf Station.

'What would be the point of that?' said Terry.
'Then you wouldn't be able to use the station,
and all the offices of Canary Wharf would be
on their side.'

'No, I don't think he was advocating that we actually do it, he was just pointing out that it would fit.'

'Hmm . . . but you'd have to take the tower apart to get it down here. And that would be an incredibly expensive business.'

We'd passed the last station before the river, and there was a heavy silence as we entered the next section of tunnel. Soon there were a few clues that we were close to where maintenance staff had been working. An abandoned high-visibility vest. Fresh bits of discarded bread crust between the rails. A brand new section of cabling yet to be turned dusty grey. Perhaps we were already under the mighty Thames? And then I knew we were there. The narrow tunnel suddenly opened out into a larger cavernous section where there was a forest of scaffolding and unwieldy machines and brightly coloured signs about site safety. And above us was a huge curved metal plate in the roof of the tunnel, clearly brand new and painted a rusty-coloured red, with massive bolts and supporting pillars. And it was dry. Everything above us was dry; there was no collapsing river tunnel here, we had taken the right decision. All of us were thinking the same thing.

'Yes!' declared Jim in relief as much as triumph. The previously silent wife of the nervous Yorkshireman burst into tears.

'Don't worry, dear,' said her husband. 'We're going to be all right. And we won't be coming back to London again.'

Caroline caught my eye, but there was nothing triumphalist in her expression: everyone was just grateful that we had not walked for an hour directly into the epicentre of the disaster.

Dreams are as much about emotions as events, and for myself the feeling was a complex sense of being ashamed of being vindicated. I had betrayed what I had thought I had believed and yet it had been the right choice.

'Looks like you were 100 per cent wrong then, Professor Stalin,' said Terry, turning on my companion. 'If we'd gone the way you wanted we'd probably all be drowning at Waterloo around now.'

Anthony gave an apologetic shrug. I wanted to come to his defence but there was no argument I could summon to contradict this terrifying thought.

'Look, we haven't got time for an inquest just yet,' I said. 'We're all relieved this tunnel strengthening seems to be sound. But it's nearly high tide, we should keep going until we are safely above ground at Canning Town.'

One or two of the phone torches were beginning to fade. The shadowy faces were growing dimmer.

'I just think grandpa here should own up that he could have killed us, that's all. We were right and you were wrong. Admit it.'

'Professor Stalin' went to speak but was interrupted.

'Look,' said Jim. 'Light!'

I knew it could not be daylight, but it still represented some kind of hope. Then we heard voices down there too: we were not alone! We called back to them and said we were on our way. Was this a rescue party? Some of the engineers, perhaps? The light grew more distinctive as we got closer, and I felt my hopes of rescue rising. Except there was something curious about the way it shone from below rather than from above.

'Weird. It's like a reflection,' said Caroline.

'How could it be a reflection?'

'Oh no! Oh my God! Oh my God, no!' said Jim. The telephone torches were directed at the ground. And their light bounced back and shimmered in the growing puddles of river water forming around our feet.

6

I had not expected to meet Margaret Thatcher in a tunnel on the Jubilee Line extension. And yet here she was: the very woman who caused this Underground route to exist, the icon of radical Conservatism and the towering bogey figure of my youth, right here beside me at the greatest moment of crisis. So this is where my journey into capitalism's *Heart of Darkness* had always been leading: finally I was face to face with liberal England's very own Colonel Kurtz. Margaret Hilda Thatcher, Conservative Prime Minister, 1979–1990.

And this wasn't the frail and powerless shadow

of the woman from that Meryl Streep film: this was the iconic Iron Lady at the height of her powers, the plutonium blonde; dressed in blue with a sturdy handbag probably containing a large brick. And maybe a small bottle of school milk that she'd snatched from an inner-city child.

At first I hadn't quite believed that it really was her as I headed towards the light and the voices: she had been standing directly in front of one of the temporary arc lights that were still illuminating this section of the engineering works. It was as if the rays seemed to emanate directly from her steely blonde hair. After so long in darkness, I squinted and averted my gaze. And then my eyes adjusted and I saw that it really was my personal nemesis, and I found myself squinting more than ever. Stranded there with her were a few ordinary members of the public who looked both frightened and worn down in equal measure. One of them looked as if drowning might be a welcome relief from the conversation they had endured before we got there.

'Look at that!' said Mrs Thatcher, pointing to the water streaming down the walls. 'The Victorian entrepreneurs built tunnels that have lasted 150 years and this section built under Mr Blair for his Dome is already leaking!'

I didn't have the energy to engage with this point – none of us could quite face going through the arguments all over again.

'If this tunnel was someone's private property, do you think they would have let it get into this state? No! No! No! They would have protected a valuable personal asset and taken more pride in its appearance!'

She never stopped coming up with new policy ideas. After you'd bought your council house, you could purchase your own private section of tube tunnel.

Her presence here convinced me that this must be the end for me. This was my cosmic punishment for having betrayed my political principles. It was not enough that I was going to drown down here; no, my very last moments would have to be spent enduring a lecture on household thrift by Margaret bloody Thatcher.

And now I felt even more foolish and hypocritical for having made what was clearly the wrong choice back on the train. The shame was actually a stronger sensation than the fear. I had espoused one set of views but acted in accordance with another. I may have always optimistically talked 'left', but when it came to a moment of real crisis, when I was under the sort of pressure that reveals a person's *deep* character, I had turned right.

How could I have lost sight of that simple inescapable truth that my personal interests and the needs of society as a whole would ultimately be the same thing? How many religions and philosophies down the millennia have reiterated the same simple principle: that happiness, inner peace and *basic human survival* depend upon thinking of your fellow man, co-operating and doing unto others as you would be done to. Jesus, Buddha, Mohammed, Confucius: you get the sense that none of them would have been in a particular rush to join the Young Conservatives.

'This doesn't prove anything,' I overheard Caroline saying to Terry. 'For all we know, the tunnel at Westminster might be leaking as well.'

'The announcement specified one tunnel. You were the one who said we should go this way. This is *your* fault,' he said.

'It's the fault of all of us,' I interjected. 'We each made a personal decision to come this way. We heard the reasons why we might go in the other direction and we each made a choice.'

'Durr!' said Terry's wife, banging her fist on her forehead to indicate my stupidity. 'But *she* told us to come this way, so it's *her* fault. Honestly, some people . . .'

The scene of this disaster was now clear to see. Water was spraying in from holes in a concrete plate on a section more on the side of the tunnel than the roof. The puddles under our feet were already rising above the soles of our shoes. Suddenly a small section of concrete fell away and the volume of water pouring into the tunnel increased. All of our instincts were telling us to rush away from the scene of this disaster as quickly as possible: in any direction, it didn't really matter, we just had to get out of there before the entire River Thames came crashing down upon us. But now came another greater test for each of us.

'Everybody listen!' shouted Jim. 'We are *not* going to have time to get out of the tunnels. Trust me, I know what I am talking about. The water is coming in through those little holes, and they're getting bigger and bigger. Before long it will be a torrent. But if we all stay and block as many holes as we can, we might be able to hold off the collapse until after high tide has peaked.'

There was a split second as everyone processed what Jim was asking of us: to stay put in what appeared to be the most perilous place we had ever been.

'No way! We're getting out of here,' barked the Yorkshireman. 'Come on, dear, we're not staying in bloody London a minute longer than needs be.'

'You can't go!' Jim was pleading now. 'For any of us to survive, we *all* have to stop the water getting in.'

In the intensity of that moment my brain seemed to process many things at once. I saw the desperate look in Jim's eyes, imploring us to have the courage to stay and work together to save the tunnel and ourselves. I heard the echoey spray and drips of water filling up our underground cave. I saw a Health and Safety sign about wearing the right sort of protective gloves. And then I felt myself moving towards Jim and taking up position beside him.

This time I had barely hesitated. I'd understood completely what had to be done: now I was putting my thumb over a leaking hole and the heel of my other hand over a smaller crack. Would we be the only two? Each person there had to make an instant judgement call: not just on whether they should do the right thing, but also on whether they could trust everyone else to do the right thing as well. Surely, I thought, this would be where the inherent self-interest and survival-of-the-fittest ideology of the right-wingers would manifest itself most clearly? And sure enough, without even pausing to see what his wife was doing, Terry began running as fast as he could back in the direction from which we had come, while his wife ran after him, repeatedly calling him a bastard.

Other anxious faces looked ready to leave. Eyes were averted; bodies subtly shifted to put themselves out of our sight-line: I could feel that the psychological tipping point had already gone against us. Then, who should come to the rescue but the very last person I would ever have expected to make the right political and moral choice. 'Come on, everyone, you heard what he said!' declared Mrs Thatcher. 'We must all do our bit; everyone must pull together!' And she hung her handbag on a cable hook and placed her body right beside me against the leaking wall.

'Why are you looking so surprised?' said Anthony, who was taking his place on my other side. 'She spent a lifetime in public service. We may have disagreed with her, but her motives were sincere. She didn't become Prime Minister so she could steal gold from the Bank of England. She believes that things can be changed and that we all have a duty to make it happen.'

The Yorkshireman repeated his assertion that they were leaving, but now his wife quietly said, 'No.' She had not spoken until now, and even her husband seemed surprised to discover that she had this ability.

'What do you mean, "no"?'

'Mrs Thatcher's right. I'm staying to help . . . And so should you.'

'That's right, up you step,' said Mrs T. 'You go there . . . why don't you move along a bit and make room for this lady? That's right . . .' And before long she was marshalling the operation, cajoling the ditherers to take their places against the threatened tunnel wall. Jim had placed his legs against the rail and then pushed against the damaged section with his back, so that he could support the wall and slow down a leak with the palm of his hand. Mrs Thatcher was now making sure that everyone else was doing likewise. The majority had stayed and it was because she had persuaded them.

And in that moment I felt an enormous gratitude towards Margaret Thatcher. After everything that had happened, she had finally come good. It seemed that the world wasn't just divided by ideologies; it was also divided between those who tried to make a difference and those who couldn't be bothered. The individuals on the train who had spoken out for one ideology or the other – Jim and Marek, Caroline and Anthony – they were the first to try and save the tunnel. Those who had not been interested in the debate had slunk away. Right now this seemed a more significant division than the one between left and right.

My feelings of enormous goodwill and gratitude towards Mrs Thatcher lasted several whole seconds, between her taking up her position, right up to when she started making casual chit-chat with me.

'This is like everyone mucking in during the war, isn't it? Or miners rescuing their comrades after a pit accident.'

Why did she have to mention the *miners* of all people?

'I think the miners were a wonderfully courageous group of people,' she continued. 'A pity the coal mines had to be closed; I thought it was a dreadful shame when they did that.'

'*They? They?* Who is this "they"?' I wanted to scream.

'Yes, the British people are always best at times of crisis. Look at everyone volunteering and doing their bit. That's what made us *Great* Britain.'

And I looked along the line to see the determined efforts of Marek from Poland and that quiet Asian student and the Turkish lady who was still hoping to get to Stratford.

'Come on, everyone, put your backs into it,' she barked in case anyone was thinking of malingering. 'Do you know the charming fable of the little Dutch boy putting his finger in the dyke?' she said to me. I forced a weak smile and nodded. I was in some physical discomfort as I pressed against the soaking tunnel wall, but this was nothing compared to my social awkwardness. 'As a young girl I wondered what it would be like to stick my finger in a dyke . . .'

I could see Jim and Caroline suppressing giggles, but she carried on blithely unaware. Now my nightmare took a horrific Freudian detour, as Mrs Thatcher unwittingly bombarded me with one sexual innuendo after another.

'Look here, my hole needs a bigger finger in it. You're a man, why don't you stick your finger in my hole?' said that familiar bossy voice. She was completely oblivious to the fact that everyone around us was biting their lips and desperately suppressing laughter.

'Now your hole is tighter,' she decided, as she fixed my gaze with those infamous blue eyes, 'So I should put my finger in yours!'

And then everyone else erupted into noisy howls of laughter and she looked around, confused and slightly hurt.

'What? What is it?'

They were laughing too much to answer her.

'So many people think I am ridiculous or dreadful,' she confided to me, 'one begins to wonder if it's really true.'

'Oh no, not at all,' I heard myself say. 'I mean, maybe a few people back when you were Prime Minister . . .'

'Oh!' She seemed surprised. 'Did people not like me in the 1980s?' she enquired anxiously.

'Erm . . .' My embarrassed pause had already given away the answer.

'I mean, did they think I was a bit uncaring?' she continued. 'A bit hectoring?'

'Well . . . *a bit*, maybe.'

Mrs Thatcher was very upset by this. 'Oh *no*, really? How uncaring, exactly? I mean like, just a little bit thoughtless, or "That heartless bitch doesn't care at all about the sufferings of the millions on the dole queues"?'

'Well, you know. Somewhere between the two, perhaps?'

She seemed mortified by this revelation:

she was far more insecure in real life than she had ever come across on the television. And in a cowardly way, this was what gave me the courage to finally confront her about all the damage that she and her successors had done. I knew it never makes any difference, but I thought I'd regret it if I didn't seize this opportunity to get it all off my chest.

'Mrs Thatcher, you know the financial crash, today's global meltdown, the water pouring into this tunnel on your Jubilee Line extension – it all proves one thing . . .'

She looked me right in the eye but amazingly didn't interrupt me. 'You should never have deregulated the City. Capitalism can't just be let off the leash, ordinary people need protection, the state has a major role to play and must intervene where necessary.' I thought I detected a slight nod of the head, so I thought, hell, I'm just going to go for it. 'The fact is, Maggie . . . left is right and right is wrong.'

This was my dream, and I am pleased to report that to the Iron Lady's credit she was now prepared to agree with me and concede that she had been completely wrong *about everything*.

'Oh God, what was I doing,' she said. 'You were right about it all and I was completely wrong. The stations along the Jubilee Line prove it. See how they illustrate the inescapable truth: capitalism oppresses the majority.'

'But Mrs Thatcher –' interjected Caroline.

'Shut up, I'm talking' – and there was a flash of the old Iron Lady. 'Oh God,' she groaned, 'I should have listened to that Neil Kinnock more, he was the only one talking any sense. And Dennis Skinner. He had actually worked as a miner you know, he knew what it was like in those communities. There *is* such a thing as society.' Her head was shaking with remorse. 'Oh God, looking at it all from your point of view, I can now see what an utter disaster my Tory decade was, and how I was the worst prime minister in charge of the worst government *ever*.'

People weren't laughing at her any more.

In fact they all seemed rather stunned to hear Mrs Thatcher talking like this.

'Yes,' agreed Marek. 'Now I see that so-called "socialism" in Poland was not socialism but state capitalism imposed by an imperial superpower.'

'Exactly,' said Mrs Thatcher. 'What you wanted was neither Washington nor Moscow but international socialism. Vote Labour but build for a socialist alternative.'

'Actually,' said Caroline. 'When you put it like that, I realize now that we Conservatives *have* been fundamentally wrong in our approach to everything . . . I now see the error of my ways and will be joining Mrs Thatcher in the Socialist Workers Party and selling newspapers outside Tesco Metro on Saturday mornings.'

'It's true,' said Roger Scruton. Hello? Where did he suddenly come from? I thought he disappeared up the tunnel hours ago. 'This journey has taught me that Karl Marx's basic analysis of profit capitalism is still applicable

today. Oh, and Chomsky's right. I do fight
like a girl.'

For someone on the left such as myself, more
used to defeats than victories, I have to say
this all added up to an extremely gratifying
moment. Everyone in the tunnel agreed that
my politics were right and theirs had been
completely wrong. All of us had seen the
evidence with our own eyes: this privatized
tunnel repair was dangerously inadequate, but
with our altruistic socialist co-operation we
would save the tunnel wall and the lives of our
comrades. My mistake was to point this out
loudly to everyone before we were actually safe.

'Please?' said the Turkish lady. 'Soon,
Stratford?'

'Yes,' I assured her. 'We'll be in Stratford
very soon.'

'Good. I want see Shakespeare's house . . .'

The collapse was quite sudden. A metal
brace above us groaned and then popped
its rivets and sprang forward with enormous
force, missing all of us but releasing tonnes

of filthy water into the tunnel. Jim had said it would need every single one of us to stay and support the wall – and because that hadn't happened, the structure behind us fractured and water came through with all the force of the sluices on the Suez Canal. I remember seeing Marek being sent crashing forward as a powerful tsunami of river water and clay cast him into the mire. But a split second later all of us were thrown into the torrent and I found myself being swept along this filthy flume, one leg painfully striking a rail or tunnel brace as I spluttered and splashed and struggled to keep my head above water. I was already twenty yards further down the tunnel when I saw another head slipping beneath the slurry.

'Mrs Thatcher – grab my hand!' I shouted. I had to save her. My body span around with the force of the swirling water, but I reached out again and nearly made contact.

'There's no point,' she spluttered as her hand fell away, 'Everyone hates me anyway . . .'

'No they don't, Mrs Thatcher. They love you.

Everyone loves you. I love you, Mrs Thatcher! I love you.'

'No,' she said. 'It's the end of the line . . .' Her head bobbed below the water, then came back up again. 'This is the end of the line.'

And more water splashed in my face as she pushed me away and disappeared below the churning foam.

'It's the end of the line! Oi, mate, wake up!' said the guard at Stratford Station. 'It's the end of the line! Give his boat race another splash from your water bottle. That normally wakes them up.'

And my eyes blinked open to see an empty Jubilee Line train with a couple of London Transport employees standing over me and chuckling as a few drops from a water bottle were gently splashed in my face.

'Oi, mate, time to get off! This is the end of the line.'

'What?'

'This is Stratford. You were asleep.'

'Mrs Thatcher?'

'Yeah. That's me. And this is Ronald Reagan. Excuse the water-boarding treatment, but we'd tried prodding you and shaking you and you don't want to go all the way back along the Jubilee Line, do you now?'

They were definitely right about that. I apologized and staggered out on to the platform, blinking and still feeling the panic and confusion of my dream. Then I stopped and thought to myself, 'I just told Mrs Thatcher that I loved her,' and I felt the need to sit down for a while.

I wandered out of the station and followed the crowds into Stratford City Westfield. The enormous shopping mall looked different seen through the eyes of a man who had just had the capitalist system explained to him by his subconscious. It seemed to be a monument to the gods of unnecessarily spending money. Branded shop after branded shop selling you things you didn't actually need but had been persuaded that you really ought to have.

Expensive trainers and novelty wrapping paper and the latest mobile phones: all being joylessly studied by people who looked exhausted at having worked so hard to earn the cash for them.

I was still feeling bleary and a little disorientated and needed a coffee. And there, queuing right in front of me, was Caroline from my dream. She was a real person: I realized she'd been sitting opposite me when I'd fallen asleep.

'You woke up then?' she said with a smile at the counter. 'You were talking in your sleep. The whole carriage was giggling.'

'Oh no, really? I had this terrible dream that society had collapsed and we were in this sort of epic capitalist disaster.'

'Oh dear!' She gestured to the busy shopping centre outside. 'Well, everything looks pretty good to me.'

'Really? I was just wondering if maybe it wasn't a dream. Maybe I did die down there and have gone to hell.'

'Gone to hell? she said, looking surprised. 'This is the biggest shopping centre in Europe. I think you mean "gone to heaven"!'

'Starbucks Rewards card?' asked the lady behind the counter.

I nearly went straight back to the platform to kill myself. I just couldn't bear the idea of Jubilee Line information describing me as a 'customer'.

'You know what this dream is telling you?' said my wife that evening.

'That I really do love Mrs Thatcher?'

'You have to leave your job and do something worthwhile. You hate your work, you hate getting on the Jubilee Line every day with all the other lemmings and doing your bit to keep the whole rotten system going.'

'You're right. I'm going to pack it in tomorrow.'

She gave me a surprised look.

'No, OK, tomorrow would be mad if I lose a month's pay by not giving the statutory notice.'

'And then?'

'Well, actually, if I'm going to stay a month, I might as well stay two months to get my Christmas bonus.'

' "None are more hopelessly enslaved than those who falsely believe themselves to be free",' she quoted back at me.

But I was determined that things would not continue as they had before. The Jubilee Line had showed me the way. I had seen how our political and financial system had evolved to keep exploiting the majority while enriching those at the very top. I had learned that politics is about the choices you make, not about the things that you say. I had seen that violence solves nothing and been shown that there is good and bad in everyone, even my greatest enemies.

And then I woke up and it had all been a dream.

PENGUIN LINES

Choose Your Journey

If you're looking for...

Romantic Encounters

Heads and Straights
by Lucy Wadham
(the Circle line)

Waterloo–City, City–Waterloo
by Leanne Shapton
(the Waterloo & City line)

Tales of Growing Up and Moving On

Heads and Straights
by Lucy Wadham
(the Circle line)

A Good Parcel of English Soil
by Richard Mabey
(the Metropolitan line)

Mind the Child
by Camila Batmanghelidjh and
Kids Company
(the Victoria line)

The 32 Stops
by Danny Dorling
(the Central line)

Mind the Child
by Camila Batmanghelidjh
and Kids Company
(the Victoria line)

The Blue Riband
by Peter York
(the Piccadilly line)

**A Bit of
Politics**

The 32 Stops
by Danny Dorling
(the Central line)

*A History of Capitalism
According to the Jubilee Line*
by John O'Farrell
(the Jubilee line)

**Musical
Direction**

Heads and Straights
by Lucy Wadham
(the Circle line)

Earthbound
by Paul Morley
(the Bakerloo line)

The Blue Riband
by Peter York
(the Piccadilly line)

*What We Talk About When
We Talk About The Tube*
by John Lanchester
(the District line)

*A Good Parcel of
English Soil*
by Richard Mabey
(the Metropolitan line)

**Tube
Knowledge**

**A Breath of
Fresh Air**

*A Good Parcel of
English Soil*
by Richard Mabey
(the Metropolitan line)

**Design for
Life**

Waterloo–City, City–Waterloo
by Leanne Shapton
(the Waterloo & City line)

Buttoned-Up
by Fantastic Man
(the East London line)

Drift
by Philippe Parreno
(the Hammersmith & City line)